P9-ECI-545

House Beautiful
container gardens

House Beautiful
container gardens

Adam Caplin

photography by Marianne Majerus

HEARST BOOKS
A Division of Sterling Publishing Co., Inc.
New York

Published by Hearst Books
A Division of Sterling Publishing Co., Inc.
387 Park Avenue South, New York,
NY 10016

First published in 2003 by Jacqui Small,
an imprint of Aurum Press

House Beautiful is a trademark owned by
Hearst Magazine Property, Inc., in USA, and
Hearst Communications, Inc., in Canada.
Hearst Books is a trademark owned by
Hearst Communications, Inc.

www.housebeautiful.com

Distributed in Canada by Sterling Publishing
c/o Canadian Manda Group,
One Atlantic Avenue, Suite 105
Toronto, Ontario, Canada M6K 3E7

Text © Adam Caplin 2003
Photography © Marianne Majerus 2003
Layout and design © Jacqui Small 2003

The right of Adam Caplin to be identified as
the Author of this Work has been asserted
by him in accordance with the Copyright,
Designs and Patents Act 1988.

All rights reserved. No part of this book may
be reproduced, stored in a retrieval system,
or transmitted, in any form or by any means,
electronic, electrostatic, magnetic tape,
mechanical, photocopying, recording or
otherwise, without prior permission in writing
of the Publisher.

Publisher Jacqui Small
Editor Bella Pringle
Designers Maggie Town, Beverly Price
Production Geoff Barlow

Library of Congress
Cataloging-in-Publication Data

Caplin, Adam.
  House beautiful container gardens /
  Adam Caplin ; photography by
Marianne Majerus.
      p. cm.
  ISBN 1-58816-254-0
  1. Container gardening. I. Title.
  SB418.C36 2003
  635.9'86—dc21

                        2003001999

10 9 8 7 6 5 4 3 2 1

Printed in Hong Kong

ISBN 1-58816-254-0

Every effort has been made to ensure that
all the information in this book is accurate.
However, due to differing conditions and
individual skills, the Publisher cannot be
responsible for any injuries, losses, and
other damages which may result from the
use of the information in this book.

contents

why containers?

Ever since I first started gardening, at the tender age of five, I was fascinated by plant pots. Small terra-cotta pots that fit into old horticultural wooden boxes were like a puzzle (a very easy one), and large plastic pots helped me imagine that I had superhuman strength as I carried three above my head.

My father was a gardener who was ahead of his time. He used plants grown in pots to change the look of the garden over a weekend, moving cacti from the greenhouse in the early summer and planting his own homegrown plants into a mixture of containers. They were small displays, filled with a few traditional bedding plants—lobelia, alyssum, and geraniums. Because our garden soil was alkaline, we grew acid-loving plants, such as rhododendrons and camellias, in large containers, so that they could sit in their preferred soil mixture.

Once I had my own garden and gardening career, trips overseas helped to broaden my mind. Not only was the food delicious in Italy, but the plants looked majestic in their old terra-cotta "homes." Large oranges and lemons spoke of impossible dreams, gnarled olive trees and oleanders seemed a distant fantasy. While on a smaller scale, old olive tins, plastic barrels, and metal containers were planted with bougainvillea, jasmine, and fragrant basil.

People brought their ideas back, and container gardening became more creative as gardeners began to take the container, and the freedom and opportunities which it allowed, seriously. The fusion of all types of influences means that it is no longer a surprise to see a fruiting lemon in the most unlikely

▶ Contemporary gardens are ideal places for containers, particularly if there are no flowerbeds or borders. These galvanized metal boxes fit in perfectly with the other landscaping materials and provide plenty of space for substantial plants, such as bamboos.

city location, or "exotics," such as oleander and bird-of-paradise, on a terrace halfway up a skyscraper. Moving these less hardy plants indoors during winter and outside again in summer is just one of the practices that are becoming familiar. Containers have helped

the gardener become more versatile with our planting and has expanded our plant vocabulary. Species that were relatively unknown or difficult to grow outside year-round have now entered the gardening vernacular.

As homes and gardens have become smaller, people have become more interested in making the most of any available space, so container gardens have grown in popularity. For a roof garden or balcony where there is no soil for planting, containers make gardening possible. These gardens often occupy difficult sites from tiny roof spaces surrounded by buildings that cast a shadow to narrow balconies and small, dark basement areas—places that may have been ignored before. Containers are a blessing for those of us with such a limited landscape.

Moving from house or apartment has also encouraged people to regard plants in containers as possessions to be taken with them to their new home. And now plants that were once considered invasive when grown in an open flowerbed, such as bamboos, can be planted up in pots and will thrive in the confined space. The result is that containers have become an important feature of the modern garden.

◀ Traditional flower borders can be given structure and atmosphere with the introduction of well-placed planted containers. Here, magnificent agaves in terra-cotta pots give focus to a large colorful border, as well as an increased sense of perspective and a classical edge.

▶ In small, courtyard gardens, containers become incredibly valuable. Here a shallow bowl is planted with small succulents and grasses to create a garden in miniature.

Planted containers are particularly valuable in contemporary gardens that are trying to establish one coherent theme. The containers act as extensions of the planting space and add impact by using more daring plantings like palms and small trees. The availability of container materials, such as more-refined concretes and galvanized metals, at affordable prices, plus larger sizes and better designs, have increased the range of containers on the market and made it easier to integrate the container with any style of garden. This doesn't need to be modern—in fact, many people like to use container plantings to re-create the atmosphere of other cultures. I still enjoy bringing a flavor of Italy into the garden by using traditional terra-cotta.

Planted containers are more than just a garden accessory. They can be joyful and uplifting, full of spring cheer and hope, they can glow like the summer sun, and they can banish the winter blues. I love the magic of plants. Combine that with the creativity of the pot maker, and you can become your own garden artist when putting the two together.

This book is intended as a guide to what is possible, to help you open your mind to the potential of planted containers in your own garden space. The planting ideas will show you how to get the most out of your containers and your plants. Whether you live out of town or on the twentieth floor of an apartment building, let your planted containers help make gardening more fun and your garden more rewarding at all times of the year.

◀ Areas that have more extreme conditions, such as this windy balcony, are much more common because of high-rise living. Lack of space means that even the smallest area cannot be overlooked. Pines in buckets help to bring nature into this most urban of settings.

▶ A difficult and dark basement garden can be transformed into a cool, relaxing area by using well-chosen plants in large containers. I particularly like the use of bold plants, like this dwarf fan palm *(Chamaerops humilis)* and arum lily *(Zantedeschia aethiopica)*, which contrast with the delicate cut leaf of an acer.

design

the setting

By choosing the most appropriate container for your outside space, in terms of the container style and choice of material, you can improve the look of your existing site and garden setting as well as making a strong display.

Containers come in so many diverse styles and materials that I still find when confronted with a good pot display that I feel a little like a child in a candy store. It is easy to get carried away when around every corner is temptation; a lovely, tall terra-cotta pot, a terrazzo square pot, or a concrete bowl, all competing for my attention. But it is important to remember that when too

many different styles of containers are placed en masse in the garden, the whole scene can appear somewhat confusing. It is better to be selective—buying the wrong containers can be an expensive mistake.

Taking the style of your house and garden into consideration will help you decide on the types of container that will look most appropriate. The backbone of

◀ The geometric patterns of this outdoor space, with its straight lines, is the perfect setting for this row of square containers. The straight stems of the black bamboo topped by soft foliage provides a link between the landscaped surfaces and nature beyond.

▼ This formal entrance is cleverly integrated with the garden. The "lollipop" topiary mirrors the box balls around the base of the steps, making a smooth transition between house and garden.

many contemporary gardens is powerful landscaping, and the garden fences, walls, and pavements often appear to be an addition to the house, enclosing the outdoor area so that it feels like an "outside room." These gardens are ruled by the desire to achieve sharp lines and clarity, so the planting plans often rely on strong foliage shapes. Finding containers that fit in with this vision helps to strengthen this effect. For example, a tall white concrete pot filled with the sharp leaves of a cordyline looks perfectly at home in a garden with white plastered walls, while square terra-cotta containers seem like a good choice for a

modern garden design based on a square grid system. To create a coherent picture, choose containers in materials that are similar to the fabric of the garden structure, in colors that complement the dominant tones. The whole impact of the design relies on a degree of control—using such heavy-duty materials as concrete or stone, clear-cut lines, containers in simple shapes, and distinct foliage.

Very formal garden spaces are dominated by structure and the use of repeated motifs—and they call for similarly systematic container plantings. Remember that the best container plans enhance what is already there and do not challenge it. A formal garden containing rows of clipped boxwood hedges, or waves of lavender, asks for simple containers with similar plantings.

Informal gardens offer a less restrictive palette and fewer limitations than modern gardens. I love the sense of time, growth, and decay, and the dominance of plants and flower borders. Here, the more traditional containers often look best, particularly the earthy colors of terra-cotta and wood, stone, and wicker, which all feel like natural occurrences in the landscape. The choice of container plants can echo the garden planting, and containers placed in borders appear as though they are growing out of the garden setting. Slight imperfections, often found with old terra-cotta and hand-thrown pots, are lovely and mirror the imperfections of nature.

Gardens created from an eclectic mixture of plants and unusual objects and materials are better equipped to absorb many different styles of containers. My own

personal favorites for a creative wild garden are recycled containers, which look as though they were born for the purpose. My own little "urban beach" garden is strewn with seashells and has several old tea chests planted with evergreens.

The main view from the house into the garden is often an important place for containers. My terrace is outside the living-room window and I have arranged my pots so that they can be seen from the inside to help integrate the indoor space with what is outside.

There are times and places where a bold container that offers a contrast to the surroundings may be appropriate. If there is an ugly view that you would like to play down, an eye-catching container can help to divert the eye. A container that stands out from its background will be seen more clearly from the house, and it can bring a forgotten area of the garden to life.

When you are looking back at the house from the garden or when containers are standing in an entrance, the house becomes the context in which the container is seen. An imposing frontage needs similarly chunky containers with real structural planting to balance its proportions. A simple, painted door provides the opportunity for a cheery planting of tulips in a glazed container, or the enthusiastic welcome of marigolds in a hand-painted terra-cotta planter. I really like to show a little bit of the personality of the home owner when choosing containers for entrance sites. Plants in pots painted by children and their friends can offer a lovely welcome. A modern frontage, which is more stylized

◀ A beautiful relaxed garden is a lovely setting for an overflow of color and growth from a copper container. This display of verbena, argyranthemum, and diascia is eye-catching and mixes well with the surrounding landscape.

▶ This sheltered urban garden is enclosed by bamboos and eucalyptus, while modern containers punctuate the space. The choice of terra-cotta blends well with the low wall, and repetition gives rhythm to the space.

◀ Walls provide an excellent opportunity for a container planting. Here, one of the most evocative of plants—a fruiting lemon tree—is trained as a wall shrub and turns the space into a Mediterranean scene. Planting the lemon tree in a container makes it easy to move the plant indoors when the weather turns cold.

▶ A little half-pot attached to the wall can add color and interest without taking up too much space or looking unbalanced.

▶▶ An old metal barrel sits in front of a vivid pink wall to create interest and perspective. The fruiting grape vine is a real treasure.

and minimal, calls out for modern terra-cotta, concrete, metal, or fiberglass.

The front of the house is an area that you see throughout the year at the entranceway to your home. It frustrates me to see flimsy containers full of half-dead bedding plants at entrances looking somewhat disappointed to see you leave, and equally disappointed when you arrive back. For a welcoming entrance, choose a large, heavy container and plant it with something similar to the evergreen *Pieris formosa* 'Wakehurst,' which flowers in spring, or a camellia if the entrance site is shady, or perhaps aromatic evergreen herbs if the site is sunlit.

roof gardens and balconies

On a practical note, roof gardens and balconies often require lightweight containers, not only because of these structures' load-bearing restrictions, but also to make carrying the pots up any stairs, and out onto the roof, easier. The choice of container may be governed by the setting. In an area where a roof terrace is surrounded by older-style brick buildings, I've seen terra cotta, old cast-iron bathtubs, and aged wood work well, while in an urban roof terrace setting surrounded by modern building structures of glass, steel, and concrete, galvanized metal, and fiberglass containers look great.

On a veranda, wood containers made from untreated hardwoods or stained or painted softwoods can help to smooth the transition from house to garden.

Use materials for containers that mimic those of the veranda, while planting the pots with plants that suit the garden aspect and style.

awkward areas

There are areas of the garden that tend to be more difficult to plant and require containers, because there is no flowerbed space. Walls next to houses or on the patio often suffer from this problem, and this is where container plantings can help. While it is extraordinary what plants will endure, try to give the plant access to as much soil as possible to help it establish a healthy root system. If the site puts limits on the size of container, choose a deep one, because the greater the volume of soil, the greater the plant's capacity for growth; also, deep soil will retain more water. If you cannot access the site easily, consider installing an automatic irrigation system to prevent plants in awkward areas from drying out.

Walls also provide the opportunity for growing plants in hanging containers. In narrow passages and small courtyard patios, they offer what is often the only available surface for gardening. Hanging containers and half-pots are also useful for growing plants in narrow sites that people have to negotiate in order to get out into the garden proper. Choose containers made from robust materials that are free of sharp edges, to make them safe when you brush past along a passageway. Wood containers are suitable, as are galvanized metal pots with rolled edges. Plastic and fiberglass are fine, although they tend to be a little lightweight and may be blown over in strong winds.

scale

Finding the most appropriate size of container for the available space is important and will help to create realistic planting opportunities, and improve the overall appearance of the garden.

It is tempting to fill up a small space with a lot of small containers, particularly if it seems logical that the more pots you have the larger the space feels. However, this can produce the opposite effect, making a small area look desperately busy.

One of the most effective tiny gardens I've ever seen has a large-scale pot against the wall, planted with a beautiful weeping birch tree. The container appears disproportionately large for the space, taking up about 25 percent of the floor space. However, this area, which had previously been dominated by its imposing walls, was transformed and the tree in its container became the focal point. The choice of tree was key, its weeping form providing a ceiling of branches that stopped the eye from traveling too high.

A large wall really does need to be balanced by a good-sized container. It will also provide for more root space for a climber or tree and a more secure anchorage.

In any garden I try to buy the large-scale pots first, just like planting a permanent garden, where the framework plants—the trees, large shrubs, and hedges—are the most important elements. Often it is the plant effect that matters most—a large plant may be required to provide screening and a focal point on a hard surface and the

pot size has to fit with the scale of plant. A tree, large bamboo, or a palm will need a large container for cultural reasons, to provide stability, and to create a balance between the plant and the container.

If the most important feature of the space is the view out of a window, then a container using small compact plants is ideal, particularly if you don't want to block that view. Often, a view simply needs underlining with plants.

An intimate space in a larger garden can look cozy with smaller pots on a table in a corner, planted with *Primula auriculas*, rock garden plants, and herbs. Placing the plants near where people stop means that you can study the beauty of the flower.

A couple of larger containers at the end of the garden can enliven a view. One of my most substantial pots is nestled at the back tucked into a verdant corner. It can only just be seen from the terrace and helps create some mystery, making people curious and wanting to explore further.

On a practical note, if you are buying a large pot for the garden, think of access and weight. It is important to check that the new container can get into the garden and that the weight of a fully planted and watered container isn't dangerous if load-bearing is an issue.

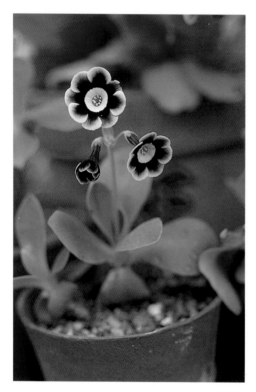

▲ Small terra-cotta pots help to highlight and set off the beauty of an individual delicate flower such as this *Primula auricula*.

◀ Using large containers and some substantial plants such as phormiums, hostas, and acers helps to reduce the impact of the wall and makes a small space look much bigger.

grouping and repetition

The grouping and repetition of planted containers can help to create an integrated scene that has dramatic impact and is harmonious, compared to the low-impact effect of scatttering them around the terrace or garden.

Gardens have often relied on containers as focal points, a single urn in the center of a circle or a pair of urns announcing the transition from the landscaping of the terrace to the soft greens of borders and lawn. However, a group of containers can transform the garden, creating a fuller and more all-year-round effect, where a single planter might look a little lost and ineffectual.

In a small space, particularly where the flowerbed space is limited, a group of containers not only looks dramatic, but provides far more planting opportunities.

A wall against paving that would otherwise be bare can become a backdrop for containers and plants. Informal groupings of containers can work well, particularly if the background is monotonous, because the contrasting styles of containers can be really eye-catching and help to liven up a dull view.

In a tiny space, restricting the styles of container is easier on the eye than an informal mixed grouping. As with all of these choices, it's really a matter of taste. Collectors and people who can't help adding more and more things to the garden and house probably get

◀ A set of similar bowl-shaped containers look natural when placed together in a group. Plant them with succulents, such as sedums and sempervivums, to highlight the harmony of the group and to help create a coherent display that is both interesting and comforting.

▶ A more eclectic mix of grasses and palms provides a variety of interest and helps to draw attention away from the fencing. Grouping them together in a haphazard way makes the display seem more relaxed and informal.

as much pleasure from the hunt for containers and plants as from planting them, and they are far more likely to have an eclectic mixture, which can be charming and fits in with their personal style.

In a contemporary garden, the use of pot repetition helps perspective and harmony. A border interrupted by a series of identical tall containers feels like a mixture of the classical and modern, with pedestals for plants surrounded by flowers and foliage. These displays can also make the garden appear longer or wider if arranged either along the length of a flowerbed or if taken across the end of the space. Visual tricks can also be used. By placing two similar style containers, one in the foreground and a smaller one in the distance, you can use perspective to create the impression of a larger garden. Repetition will often involve putting containers in flowerbeds, and this is both delightful and challenging, because it gives the impression that the containers have become an integral part of the planting.

Grouping similar containers together can be a comforting and beautiful feature. Similar plantings tend to fit well in a group like this. I avoid having too much color in any one pot, because I find that they can end

up looking too "corporate," which I dislike. The whole effect of a group of similar pots should be like a beautiful painting, a harmony of foliage, flowers, shapes, and materials.

Windowsills, balconies, and roof gardens have a more practical need for grouping, because there is no flowerbed space. Individual pots grouped together help to protect each other, particularly in a windy position. A wind-tolerant plant, such as a bamboo, in a larger container can act as protection for smaller, more delicate plants. A compact basil in front of a larger pot gets enough protection in the summer to grow and crop well. This has the added impact of using some of the containers as backgrounds for others. Terra-cotta makes a great foil for smaller containers with earthy hues. Grouping also enables you to water more easily. I try to keep real moisture lovers near each other and those that prefer dry conditions together as well.

Planted containers on windowsills should reflect the style of the house—a contemporary house requires complementary containers. The group will often benefit from repetition of simple pots and plants, because this fits in with the lines and symmetry of the house. Older houses

◀ Herbs grown in identical containers look very reassuring and wholesome. I love the way the different growing habits of the plants really show themselves off from the laid-back catmint in the foreground to the feathery fennel at the back.

▲ On a windowsill, where space is limited, using similar pots makes sense. Too much of a mix might appear chaotic, and planting them all with skimmia offers diversity without confusion.

often require a similar treatment to avoid disturbing the front. I choose plants and containers in muted colors.

Repetition can also be reassuring, offering a point of reference, particularly if it is difficult to see where the boundary begins and ends. That is why using controllable and reliable evergreens like box and pittosporum, and the architecture of powerful evergreens, such as phormiums and bamboos, can help to mark out your territory.

The more informal the garden, particularly if a lot of different types of plants and materials are used, the more informal the grouping of containers can be. My garden had at least three major groupings: one for edibles in mixed containers, another for shade-loving plants, and the last for a few odd plants in recycled objects.

A group of containers in view from a living-room window can be a beautiful addition to the garden picture, and it is here that containers can be at their most flexible. I love to be able to change this picture once in a while to make sure that these groups are always looking their best. I grow some perennials in plastic containers, which are then slipped into more attractive permanent pots when the flowers are budding, then moved into a less prominent position when out of flower. One group of pots has an agapanthus for summer and the fall (the seedheads look splendid in the fall), skimmia for the fall and winter, a group of *Primula vulgaris* for early spring, and hostas for spring and early summer.

▼ These clipped boxwood shapes in large galvanized metal containers work well set against this panoramic cityscape. Their shape gives a sense of solidity and "grounding" to this high-rise terrace.

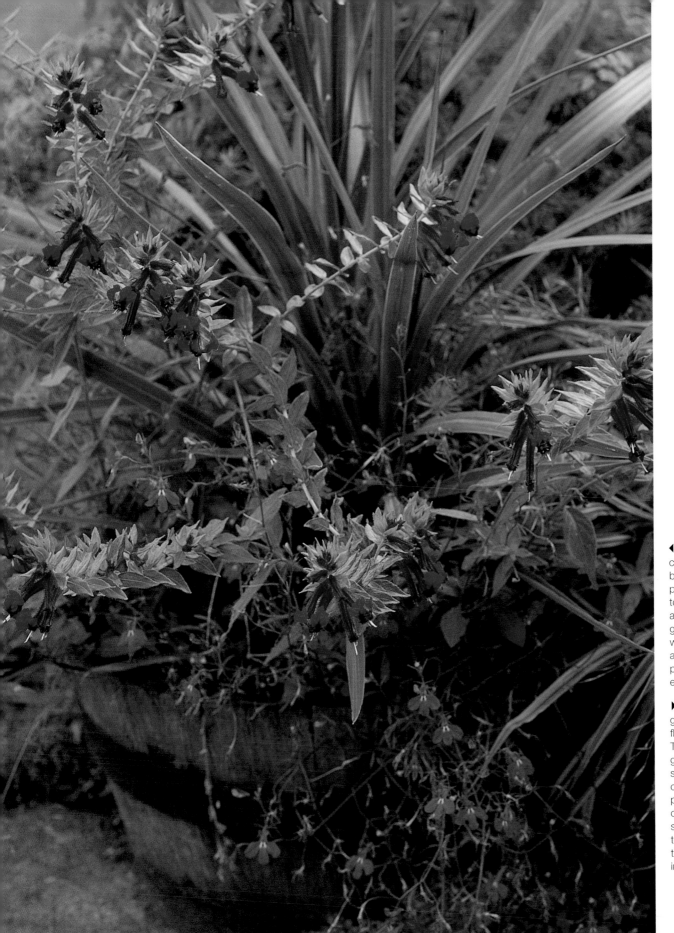

◀ This display of hot colors, with red cuphea, blue lobelia, and purple phormium, has a warmth to it and bursts out like a natural explosion of generosity from this wooden barrel. Flower and foliage colors can produce powerful emotional effects.

▶ I like the idea of being greeted by this cheerful flowering window box. The petunias and geraniums offer a stunning color combination and produce huge quantities of flowers throughout the summer. Although the tonal range is modest, this display appears incredibly opulent.

color

Containers now come in a dazzling and bewildering range of colors, offering the gardener more choice and potentially more confusion. How do you select the colors that are most suited to your garden space?

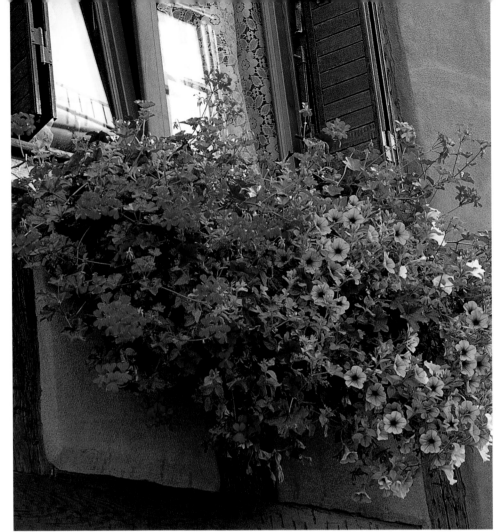

I remember my own excitement in the 1980s on first seeing the colorful new glazes on containers imported from the Far East. I planted a red-leafed Japanese maple in a brown dragon-pattern pot to re-create a little bit of the Orient in a shady corner of the garden, and white trumpet lilies in the dark-blue glazed stoneware pot. The following year, glazed terra-cotta became fashionable, and the fresh cream colors looked lovely planted with pale violas. By the time shiny galvanized metal window boxes made an appearance, my garden had started to look like a mixed collection of work in an art gallery—interesting when the containers were seen in isolation, but with no sense of unity.

Colorful containers, both machine- and handmade, that make use of the various stone and terra-cotta glazes, look wonderful planted simply and even better if they match something already planted in the garden. Pink glaze stoneware, for example, can look lovely sited near a pink flowering quince, while the grays and blacks of concrete and stone containers work well in a modern garden alongside dark purple cotinus.

In general, warm colors tend to be passionate and intense, while cooler colors are more relaxing. I love the bright, vibrant colors of the Mediterranean—old painted barrels full of bright begonias and bright plastic buckets—all framed by the sunlit glow of a whitewashed wall. The sheer exuberance of the scene is like a celebration of life. The temptation on returning home is to re-create this mood, filling up brightly colored containers with shocking purples, intense blues and joyful yellows. However, the bright colors that expressed themselves so clearly against the blue sky and bright sun appear less vivid in northern temperate climates and, sadly, it is hard to re-create the same feeling.

In shade, use pale plant colors to help lighten the atmosphere. Pastel shades will look more natural than bright colors, because they reflect the small amount of light that is available. Choose containers from a range of natural colors—pots that blend in with the background and do not stand out too much. Darker foliage and flower colors can be useful to enhance the feeling of reflective melancholy in shady areas. Ferns and other dark, leafy foliage, such as fatsia and *Viburnum davidii*, are ideal, as are shade-loving flowers such as periwinkles (*Vinca* species). Keep the pot color dark, or use old materials, such as stone, and encourage the pots to grow moss and to weather.

▼ A pyramid of red, orange, and primrose-yellow *Ipomoea lobata*, and the fiery coral red flowers of *Fuchsia* 'Thalia.' These two look perfectly at home in front of a glorious display of climbing clematis.

▶ Individual concrete containers bring a touch of artistry to the garden. This one is like an abstract painting with its purple base rising to its gold-green top of mind-your-own-business (*Helxine soleirolii*).

One advantage of container gardening is that you can use pots to add color to the garden and they are portable. A predominantly green background might benefit from a pale yellow splash of nicotiana flowers, or the blue-gray leaves of *Hosta sieboldiana*. A sunny area can be transformed by introducing a blazing red-flowered salvia, or plants with soft gray and silver foliage, such as lavenders, *Convolvulus cneorum,* or the simple cut-leaved cineraria. The neutral tones offered by silver and gray foliage will fit in with virtually any container material, including galvanized metal or bleached wood.

I think that limiting the color palette for your choice of container and plants is worthwhile, because there is a formidable range of tones in any single color. Blue-flowered plants range from the startling intensity of *Ceanothus* 'Puget Blue' through to the gorgeous pale blue of *Clematis* 'Perle d'Azur.' The deep reds of *Clematis* 'Ernest Markham' contrast with the wonderful burgundy of *Pelargonium* 'Lord Bute.' Even white varies enormously—my favorite white shrub is *Exochorda* x *macrantha* 'The Bride.' More recently, new bedding plants have increased the available palette. I particularly like the range of mauve and blue verbenas and the attractive and diverse half-hardy salvias and penstemons.

The most prominent color in gardens is green, which comes in almost every shade. Use these differences when planting your pots. Chamomile gently spilling over a terra-cotta rim in front of a darker green background of foliage is an extremely comforting picture.

Solid blocks of color grown in containers appear more substantial, particularly in contemporary garden settings. Here, I tend to mix fewer plants to achieve more striking results. Foliage color is extremely important. The black grass *Ophiopogon planiscapus* 'Nigrescens' is stunning in a container, as is the fabulous range of coleus leaf colors.

As the year advances, the pattern of the sun changes. In my city garden, the terrace is in partial shade by midsummer as the branches of an overhanging tree come into full leaf, so I move containers with bright-colored flowers to the sunniest position and also move those that need the sun to ripen their fruits, such as tomatoes and eggplants.

Favorite colors are as important in the garden as they are in the house and can be used to create harmony between indoor and outdoor spaces. I like to carry some of the interior colors outside, as well as bring some of the exterior inside. My indoor container is the smaller version of the one just outside the main window and is painted in the same sandstone color. The little citrus tree inside the living room helps to integrate the scene, and the colors look gorgeous.

texture

Natural plant textures help to add character to the garden, creating interesting effects in all four seasons. Containers can complement these textures and act as a foil for flowers and foliage to show them off to best advantage.

Containers add many unique textures that would otherwise be missing in the garden, from the fine-grained look of terra-cotta to the hard reflective surface of zinc. Containers not only bring their own textures but also act as a foil for foliage and flowers, high-lighting, complementing, and contrasting with different parts of the plant structure. For example, the soft foliage of woolly thyme *(Thymus pseudolanuginosus)* creeping over the rim of a stone or concrete pot makes for a fascinating contrast. Textures help to create real depth and feeling in the garden and are an important and subtle addition to the gardener's palette.

The surfaces in a modern garden are usually prominent, relying on reflective panels and pavements, fences, walls, and platforms to create an effect. Pots can either contrast with or complement these surfaces. The starkness of a new concrete container can stand strong against a textured wall, reinforcing its solidity.

The rougher look of some materials can be used effectively, particularly the grainier surface of weathered stone, concrete, and terra-cotta. I think that it is the mixture of container and plant textures that helps to create a lovely garden, and it is by experimenting with these effects that you will introduce an extra dimension.

▲ Geometric scalelike patterns on this container create a texture which is accentuated by the spiky leaves of a sempervivum.

◀ Containers introduce important texture to the garden. This terra-cotta urn contrasts with the frothy flowers of gypsophila and shows off the structure of a trailing sedum.

aging

Some containers look more distinguished with the passing of time. Use the natural processes of weathering and aging to add character to your outdoor space.

The changing appearance of garden containers as they get older and are exposed to the elements helps to remind us that the garden is not an enclosed room but a living organic space, where it rains, gets cold, and, once in a while, the sun shines!

An old weathered pot looks so full of horticultural wisdom and character. It is such a contrast to other areas of life, where signs of wear-and-tear, such as mold on a wall or rust on the car, are so unwelcome.

Metal containers age in a variety of ways, and the contrast between brand-new metal and rust brings the most dramatic change in as little as six weeks. Copper,

when it ages, oxidizes to a gorgeous green verdigris, which is one of the most wonderful of colors in the garden.

In my garden I love rusting metal, and as a painter I often try to reproduce its warm brown tones on canvas. Rust has an interesting texture and can create a lovely background for the right plant—a purple-leaved phormium, the bronze of an acer, and the dark tones of *Pittosporum* 'Tom Thumb.'

Some metals are treated so that they do not age too quickly, particularly those made of galvanized metal and stainless steel, while others are expected to oxidize and rust with time to produce a completely different effect from new.

Containers in those metals that remain untouched by the aging process are well-suited to small modern gardens, where maintaining the glossy sheen of the material is important, because they are expected to

◀◀ An old food tin quickly ages to produce a textured rusty effect. The mottled purple leaves of heuchera are the ideal partner to create a harmonious and attractive display.

◀ The stems of black bamboo look stunning growing among the russet and brown tones of a weathered metal trough. Decay such as this in the garden is a reminder of the beauty and power of nature.

match the unchanging fabric of the house or urban landscape. Galvanized metal containers against the sleek metal and glass materials of modern buildings rely on this.

terra-cotta

Different types of terra-cotta age in different ways. Dark-colored, heavyweight, machine-manufactured terra-cotta tends to age with less grace than some of the hand-thrown pots, due to an oil that is added to the clay during production to make it more malleable. The lighter color of Vietnamese, Malaysian, and Chinese pots ages quickly. The hand-thrown, dark-colored terra-cotta clays can age beautifully, but they often take longer than Asian pots to achieve this effect.

A well-aged pot is truly magnificent, and most take about five years from new before they start to look their best.

Being impatient, I like to speed up the aging process and often buy old containers for their imperfections. You can encourage aging, particularly algae and moss growth on terra-cotta, concrete, and stone, by smearing the surface with yogurt or fresh horse manure. The best condition to encourage silvering is a sunny position. The silvering effect on terra-cotta is a result of the salts leaching out of the material.

aging wood

Wood containers decay in different ways, depending on the type of wood and where

the containers are situated. Like terra-cotta, wood will become silvered in the sun, which looks attractive, giving a seaside sun-bleached effect. Damp and shady conditions will encourage untreated wood to rot. This can be a problem for large wooden containers, because they may eventually fall apart and will also attract wood-loving insects. To impede wood containers from rotting, scorch the interior surface with a blow torch to create an inert surface that won't rot.

concrete & stone

These materials have porous surfaces that absorb water, which encourages the growth of moss and algae. To keep stone and concrete looking clean and modern, spray the surface with a transparent waterproofing sealant (available from aquatic centers) to stop the water from being absorbed.

◀◀ A mixture of containers provides plenty of opportunities to show off the different aging processes, from the silvering of terracotta to the algae and moss growth on concrete. Moss creeping over pot surfaces can soften hard edges and creates a subtle background for plants.

◀ Herbs seem to be natural partners for really well-weathered containers. I think there is a special relationship between aromatic edibles and the earthiness of older pots.

▶ The gentle silvering of old wooden produce boxes helps to create a seaside atmosphere on this roof terrace. Plants such as the blue-gray grass (*Festuca glauca*), the sea holly (*Eryngium* species), and other gray leaves help to reinforce this image.

materials

terra-cotta

There are many different types, styles and shapes of terra-cotta. Selecting pots that are going to be most appropriate for your contemporary or traditional garden is key as are the plants and planting schemes that will help the containers to look their best.

If there were only one material available to make plant containers, I would choose terra-cotta. It is rooted in horticultural tradition and some of the first-known containers for plants were made out of this natural material. One of the most beautiful and romantic gardens I have ever seen was an old derelict garden in Italy, where ancient terra-cotta containers stood proud but empty while everything else around them was gracefully falling apart.

As well as being extremely beautiful, terra-cotta provides a good home for the roots of plants. The material is naturally porous, so it supplies oxygen to the roots and also ensures good drainage. It stays cool even in the heat of the summer sun.

Nowadays, terra-cotta pots are made in Italy, France, Great Britain, the United States, and, increasingly in China and Vietnam. Each type has its own appeal and the clay from which they are made, the mixture, the finish, and the drying process all contribute to their character. Regional differences can be significant, and pots made by individual potters are distinct. Maybe that is what makes terra-cotta containers so marvelous—the slight nuances in color, the way the material ages, the texture, and the shape that all help to define their character.

◀◀ This wonderful empty olive jar appears to have been planted in a border surrounded by fennel and other sun-loving plants. You can almost feel the heat in this Mediterranean garden scene.

◀ A lime-washed jar fits into the enclosed space of a basement garden. The daisylike flowers of erigeron and white gaura intermingle to complete a light, subtle, and natural display.

▲ Terra-cotta is extremely versatile and has an important place in the modern garden. This contemporary triangular shape filled with the striking swordlike foliage of a silver astelia sits confidently in front of a rusting steel panel.

The earthy colors of terra-cotta rarely look out of place in any style of garden. Large, light, and inexpensive square and rectangular planters (now mainly imported from the Far East) are ideal for the enclosed, often rectangular smaller space of many urban gardens, roof terraces, and balconies. The traditional shapes are still lovely, and the "long tom"—so-called because it was once used to grow tomatoes—is a slender and exquisite pot that has timeless appeal. Formal gardens look elegant with topiary planted in large terra-cotta containers, more natural informal-style gardens with penstemons creeping over the edge of an aged pot, and modern gardens with the architectural dark green leaves of fatsias in large

circular clay pots. I can hardly think of a plant that does not benefit from an association with terra-cotta.

The versatility of clay also means that containers can be molded or hand-thrown in a variety of shapes. Hand-thrown terra-cotta containers are more individual, with slight variations in shape, and when placed together make a charming family group. Some of these pots, particularly from small, top-quality suppliers are very special – with prices to match. These are well suited to plants that will grow for many years in the container. Such plants as citrus, vines, olives, and figs are a natural partner for these, majestically aging together, which creates an incredible feeling of permanence.

Machined terra-cotta often has a much smoother, more regular finish and is often less expensive than hand-thrown pots. But even with machined pots, it is still possible to find some variation, and I often actually prefer slightly irregular machined pots (as long as they have not cracked during the firing process), because these have a little more character. However, if you are buying a group of pots to create a modern, symmetrical effect, machine-made pots are ideal, not only because they are inexpensive, but they are absolutely identical.

Beautiful individual pieces often deserve a special place in the garden and require less planting, because attention should focus on the pot. I can never understand the desire to cover a beautiful pot with a shaggy mop of flowers when it is the container itself that is the subject. These are often classical in shape, such as a Greek urn, or a more modern shape, such as a tall cylinder. Rhubarb forcers are one of those wonderful shapes that seem to look great whether planted or not. They were used to help force rhubarb into growth early in the season. There are also sea-kale forcers that keep the early shoots of sea kale blanched. Pots such as these give the garden an atmosphere of tradition, expertise, and earthiness, creating a happy association with the walled gardens of the past.

◀ Glazed terra-cotta pots have become a valuable addition to the garden. This green pot provides an attractive base for spring bulb displays, and its smooth surface shows no signs of aging.

▶ This subtle gray glaze tinged with lilac introduces a modern color palette to the garden. I like the calm and serene nature of this glaze, which works well with such plants as orange-petalled Icelandic poppies (*Papaver nudicaule*) and the large-leaved pineapple plant (*Eucomis* species).

◄ The finish of terra-cotta depends on the clay from which it is made. These pots are produced from a clay mined in one particular area in Zimbabwe, which gives it a unique, very grainy texture, which works well with the ornamental grasses.

▶ An updated version of the "long tom" shows how this classic and simple design has endured. This stylish sleek shape looks wonderful paired up with topiary shapes.

▼ A mature calamondin completely transforms the atmosphere of a border, introducing an exotic edge. Citrus trees are excellent partners for terra-cotta, not only looking good but appreciating the porous, free-draining nature of the material.

Glazed terra-cotta is somewhat beautiful, either completely glazed or partially to allow some of the clay to show through. I like these partial glazes, because terra-cotta is such a lovely material that it seems such a shame to cover the whole thing up.

If placing pots in gardens in cold regions, check that the terra-cotta is frost-resistant. The containers that are most vulnerable to cracking in freezing conditions are those that have been air dried. This drying technique used to be more common with pots made in Vietnam, China, and Spain, however, most are now dried in a kiln and sold with a guarantee of frost-hardiness. Guard against poor drainage by adding broken crockery to the bottom of the pot before adding the soil, and make sure there are adequate drainage holes. Soil that becomes waterlogged in a container will expand as it freezes and can cause the pot to crack.

Terra-cotta is a brittle material and may break if knocked over or if accidentally hit by a gardening tool or passing wheelbarrow. Try to avoid placing these containers in "heavy traffic areas," where there is the potential for this type of damage. Pots that have a narrow base are also far less stable than square-sided ones, so avoid putting taller plants in these containers if your site is exposed or windy.

During the summer months, sitting the base of the container in a saucer of water is a good idea. Terra-cotta is a porous material that dries out quickly and a couple of weeks unwatered in the summer may kill off the plants. Before going away, move the containers into a shady site, and sit them on saucers with a thin layer of gravel to help the plant take up water more slowly.

Pot "feet" for large containers can look splendid, and they also help to improve root aeration and drainage. I would only consider them for huge pots, particularly as they can make smaller pots unstable, and I also think that pot feet are a bit too grand for the smaller containers.

METHOD

• Plant when the danger of frost has passed.

• Place a layer of broken crockery in the bottom of the container to improve drainage and use a peat-free, multipurpose compost.

• To encourage a continuous display of flowers, ensure that the plants are well fed throughout the summer months with a liquid tomato food. Deadhead the geraniums regularly.

• Overwinter the geraniums in a light, frost-free area. 'Lotusland' requires constant warmth through the winter and is best kept in a heated greenhouse. Keep the potting compost dry and cut back hard before placing outside again in mid-spring in a frost-free site.

baked earth

This smooth, terra-cotta basin in the shape of a boulder creates a simple brownish-red base for a vibrant pink and red flower mixture. The jagged-edged variegated leaves of the geraniums hide the rim of the terra-cotta pot and help to blur the boundary between the pot and the plants. I appreciate the positive energy of this display—like fireworks bursting out of the container— and the long flowering season of both geraniums and pinks makes this dazzling arrangement rewarding.

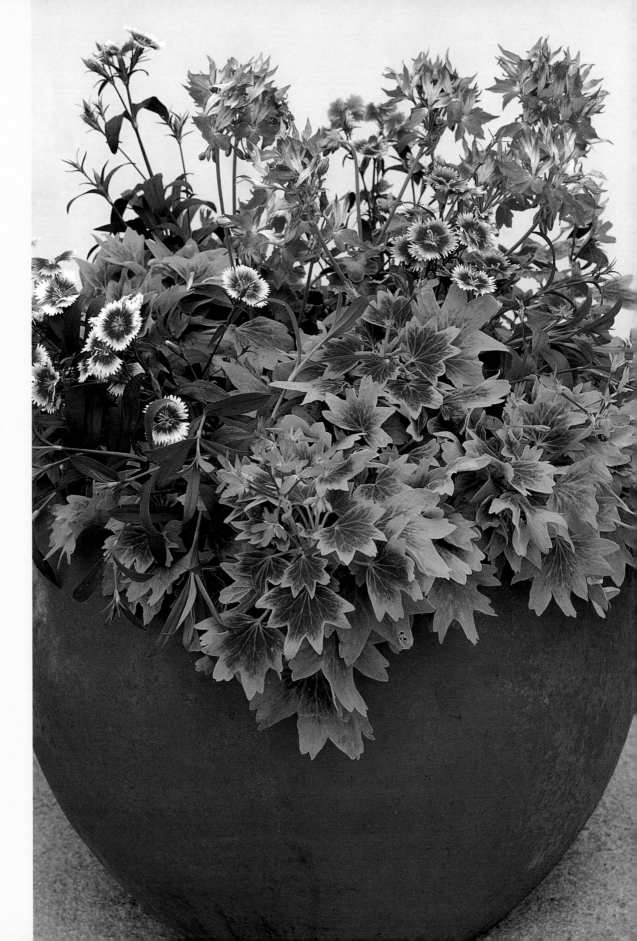

PLANTING MATERIALS

Large terra-cotta container (machine-manufactured in the Far East)

Broken terra-cotta crockery

Peat-free multi-purpose compost

PLANTS

Geranium PELGARDINI 'Lotusland'

Geranium FIREWORKS 'Salmon'

Dianthus species (With maroon-eyed, pale pink flowers with deeply fringed petals.)

PLANT ALTERNATIVES

Geranium 'Occold Shield' (golden leaf)

Geranium 'Vancouver Centennial' (purple leaf)

Plectranthus 'Sasha' (golden foliage)

PLANTING MATERIALS

Heavy-duty terra-cotta window box

Broken crockery

Soil-based compost and peat-free multipurpose compost

PLANTS

Nicotiana – green or white-flowered cultivars

Helichrysum petiolare

Linum perenne

METHOD

• Make sure that the window box has drainage holes.

• Add an equal mixture of soil-based compost and peat-free multipurpose compost. Soil-based compost adds weight and, therefore, stability to the container, and it also holds nutrients for longer.

• Plant in spring after the danger of frost has passed. Keep the plants well-watered and fed with a flower food. (This container is densely planted so will be greedy for moisture.) It will flower all summer and into the fall.

• Trim back the trailing silver helichrysum leaves if they become too overgrown and dominant in the container.

• Deadhead the nicotiana flowers as they die back to help prolong their flowering period.

country-style terra-cotta

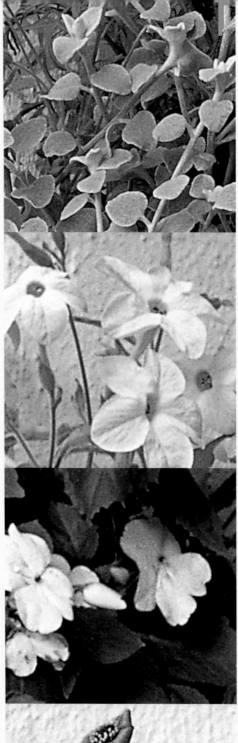

A window box when planted should look full and voluptuous, creating the effect of a miniature overgrown garden in a limited space. Window boxes, particularly when making a seasonal summer splash, should be generous and welcoming. Here, the nicotiana flowers, white busy lizzies, and vivid blue flax flowers create an informal-style planting that will brighten up an area that doesn't receive much direct sunlight. All these plants, including the silver trailing helichrysum leaves will thrive in the limited space of the container, spilling over the edges to form a full display that will last throughout the summer months and into the fall.

METHOD

• Drill drainage holes in the container base (*see* Care, *page 133*) if none are present. Add several pieces of broken crockery and plant in an equal mixture of peat-free multipurpose compost and soil-based compost.

• Plant this summer display in mid-spring when frost is unlikely to occur.

• Keep well fed with flower food. Deadhead the argyranthemum regularly to encourage the optimum number of flowers.

• Cut back lightly in the fall.

• Argyranthemums can be over-wintered in a cool, light, frost-free area such as a greenhouse or a sun room.

• Prune hard and feed the following spring before planting out once again.

summer apricots

Here, the mixture of the palmlike leaves of cordyline, half-hardy argyranthemum daisies, and seasonal plants, such as blue lobelia, orange mimulus, and salmon-pink verbena, combine well to make one arrangement. The volume of flowering plants in this container produces a spectacular display, and all these plants can survive without too much moisture, so they coexist happily. The plant combination grows best when placed in a sunny site and will last throughout the summer. The cordyline leaves are the only permanent element and act as a frame for this display. In the fall, replace the summer-flowering material with violas and pansies for winter.

PLANTING MATERIALS

Terra-cotta urn from Crete

Broken crockery

1 part soil-based compost to 1 part peat-free multipurpose compost

PLANTS

Argyranthemum

Cordyline australis 'Purpurea'

Lobelia erinus

Mimulus aurantiacus

Verbena x *hybrida* 'Salmon'

PLANT ALTERNATIVES

Brachyscome

Cordyline australis 'Sundance'

Diascia

Osteospermum

stone

Containers made from stone are magnificent and are worth giving a prominent place in the garden. They are heavy, solid, and provide a wonderful feeling of permanence. In a world where everything seems so transient and manufactured, stone is a real treat.

In a contemporary garden, stone containers can appear like part of the landscaping, fitting in well with textured concrete walls and raised beds. In a English-style cottage garden, stone containers blend seamlessly with the natural world, providing planting space for saxifrage, and the many different types of sedum.

Solid stone containers, such as old stone sinks and troughs originally used for feeding animals in Europe are extremely beautiful and worth trying to obtain. Make the container an important feature in the garden, and choose plants that will help show off its beauty. In sunny sites, fill stone troughs with rock garden plants and such compact growers as sedums, the wonderful tiny-leafed raoulia that forms a tight mat, or even some of the slow-growing conifers. These solid stone containers are heavy to transport, and you'll need help when positioning them in your chosen site. Troughs made of reconstituted stone, or "tufa"—a concrete and peat mixture—are lighter. They are inexpensive, although not a convincing alternative to the real thing.

One of the more recent introductions are stone containers called terrazzo. These have a concrete core and are surrounded by chipped stones set in resin. They are less brittle than some of the reconstituted stone containers due to this resin content. The stone is polished to produce a fine reflective surface in colors ranging from pure white to dark gray. Terrazzo containers are cast in a lot of shapes and are inexpensive.

Tall terrazzo cylinders look good in contemporary gardens, simply planted with the silver-gray of astelia foliage or the black grassy blades of *Ophiopogon planiscapus* 'Nigrescens.' Use foliage or flowers to enhance the container color but make sure that the container is not obscured by plant material.

Glazed stoneware comes in a wide range of colors and has become an important product for the modern gardener. I love some of their deep powerful blues, dark pinks, and grays, which offer a strong framework.

◀ One of the new generation of terrazzo planters made from stone chippings set in resin, the pot has a fascinating surface similar to marble. Its simplicity is enhanced by pure white tulips.

▶ A pale gray stone bowl planted with grape hyacinths looks effective, because the diminutive plants do not distract from the beauty of the bowl. A mulch of slate chippings helps to anchor the plants.

These bright container colors will set the tone for the garden, so take care when choosing them. (I prefer to use stone containers that are easy to blend with the garden design and planting plan. This is one of the strengths of neutral-colored containers.) You need to be very sure of your design when using large stone glazed containers in strong colors. These striking pots are best used as a deliberate foil for plants. Place them in a flowerbed as a solitary feature, or behind pots that have been planted. Silvery foliage, such as artemisia, planted in front of a deep blue terrazzo pot is a lovely combination.

Reconstituted stone in urn shapes that mimic designs from the past are valuable for recreating historic garden designs. They are also useful for fusing old and new styles. I have seen modern gardens where classical-shaped reconstituted stone containers create an interesting contrast to modern features. The urns often look a little too new at first, but soon weather to resemble old stone.

◀ A wonderful old stone trough has a beautiful appearance, which is worth showing off. A mixture of succulents and trailing geraniums fills the interior of the trough without covering up the front facade.

▼ Slate can make wonderful and attractive containers that fit into most styles of garden. There is something modern in both the color and the simplicity of slate. I make my own slate containers by facing plastic planters with old slate roof tiles. I have also seen this done with thin pieces of limestone, though their weight and irregular shape make this quite difficult.

METHOD

• Drill drainage holes and fill up half the pot with the broken pieces of crockery.

• Use a lightweight filler, such as broken pieces of polystyrene trays, to half-fill the pot and prevent it from becoming too heavy.

• Fill in between the pieces of polystyrene with peat-free multipurpose compost.

• Early in the season, plant 3 to 5 young coleus plants. Coleus grows quickly as summer bedding, so it will soon fill out this large pot. Trim back the stems regularly to encourage bushy growth.

• Feed with nitrogen-rich food in the summer and trim to keep the plants bushy.

• Keep the display well-watered—do not let it dry out.

pink glaze

This summer and fall display is vibrantly simple, both in the choice of plants and dark pink, glazed stoneware container, which help to set off one another. Sometimes a single species planting just can't be bettered as this colorful display shows. Early in the season, before it is warm enough to plant the coleus, you could grow such bulbs as the early spring-flowering reticulata iris to create a succession of color. You can overwinter the coleus plants by moving the container into a cool, light place, such as a greenhouse or sun room. Keep the plants relatively dry. However, they are temperamental and, even when kept in these conditions, the coleus may need replacing the following spring.

PLANTING MATERIALS

Glazed stoneware container 3 feet (1 m) tall

Broken crockery

Broken polystyrene or similar lightweight filler

Peat-free multipurpose compost

PLANTS

Coleus 'Black Dragon' (dark red leaves)

PLANT ALTERNATIVES

Other *Coleus* species

Iresine herbstii

Melissa officinalis

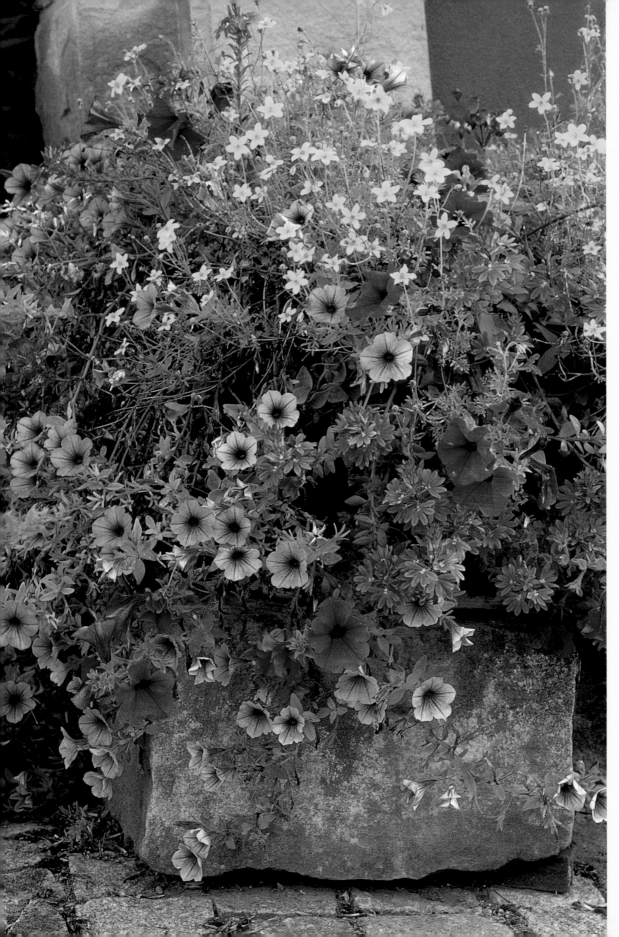

PLANTING MATERIALS

Stone trough

Broken crockery

1 part soil-based compost to 1 part peat-free multi-purpose compost

PLANTS

Bidens ferulifolia

Petunia 'Purple Wave'

Petunia 'Surfinia'

Scaevola aemula

PLANT ALTERNATIVES

Euryops pectinatus

Felicia amelloides

Tropaeolum Jewel Series (Nasturtium)

Verbena 'Sissinghurst'

METHOD

• Drilling the base of a stone container to make drainage holes is difficult, and you will need a powerful, slow drill with a masonry bit. An alternative is to use crushed charcoal and gravel for drainage, and plant the display in a plastic container inside the stone.

• Plant the display in spring using an equal mixture of multipurpose compost and soil-based compost.

• Feed the display with a flower food and cut back straggly growth during the summer, deadheading when necessary.

• In mid- to late summer when the petunias become overgrown and start to look straggly, feed them to encourage new growth and more flowers.

trailing petunia trough

Wonderful examples of such stone planters as this can be found in antique stores that specialize in old garden ornaments. However, beware of the weight—it'll need at least two people to carry it! When choosing container plants, I like to buy them in flower so that I can play with the colors to make sure that they work in harmony with the stone. Trailing *Petunia* 'Surfinia' is a new type and a good choice, because it produces an abundance of flowers over a long season, many of which are scented, and they are fairly weather resistant (meaning that the petunia flower petals don't damage easily). The darker blue-purple petals and paler blue scaevola work beautifully against the color of the stone, while the yellow bidens enliven the top of the display without interrupting the color harmony.

concrete

Plant containers manufactured from concrete have made a comeback, with different finishes and styles now available. Use concrete planters in your garden to help integrate plants with the range of landscaped surfaces that surround it.

Concrete has undergone a revival. No longer limited in its association with the gray, drab surface of buildings constructed in the 1950s and '60s, concrete has a fresh and modern appeal.

Concrete containers can be cast into almost any shape, and there is a great variety of surface finishes available, including one that allows for a smooth polished finish, the texture and color of limestone. Advances in color technology have begun to produce some inspiring new color tones and effects in concrete.

Thin-walled concrete containers are available in large, square, rectangular, or circular shapes, and they are relatively lightweight. They are suitable for roof gardens and balconies where load-bearing might be an issue. To ensure that they are strong, the thin-walled concrete is usually reinforced with fiberglass. This also makes it less brittle. Thin-walled concrete containers look slightly "retro," and can contribute to a Modernist feel. In the 1960s, thin-walled concrete planters were used in parks and public spaces, so I think that they have to be planted well to avoid associations with municipal areas.

Thicker-walled concrete containers belong to a newer generation of planters. They are easier to find and are a better value than thin-walled concrete pots. They look good in small urban gardens where there is a high proportion of landscaping material to foliage, flowers and lawn. If the garden is surrounded by buildings, walls, fences, and hard surfaces, concrete

◀ A terrace paved in concrete is the ideal setting for concrete planters. These large reinforced boxes provide space for a mix of silver and gray-leafed plants, which both fit in with the material and help to soften all the hard surfaces that surround it.

▲ Square concrete pots have a simplicity that fits in with modern design. A white-flowering datura is slipped inside the square in its own plastic pot. It will look magnificent in summer and can be brought in during the winter to be replaced by a winter-flowering display.

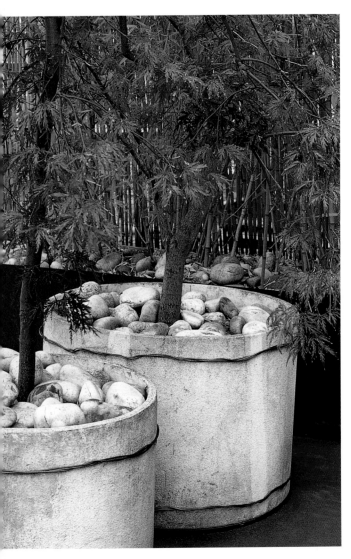

available in a greater choice of shapes, from round bowls to tall cylinders. Although heavy, they are surprisingly delicate and can easily be chipped if banged into, and their weight makes them difficult to transport. Think carefully before purchase about whether they are really appropriate for your garden, and take care that they aren't too heavy if load-bearing is an issue.

In a contemporary garden, if you want to keep concrete surfaces clear of algae and moss, scrub them with a mild detergent, or protect them by applying a clear stone waterproofing agent. A dry, sunny position will also help to inhibit algae and moss growth. Stand pale-colored concrete containers on hard ground well away from soil, which can stain the surface. If badly stained, concrete can be covered with a coat of masonry paint.

When drilling drainage holes in concrete, be patient. Use a masonry or ceramic drill bit, and place the rim of the container on a soft surface to allow a bit of "give." After planting, I like to cover the soil with a mulch of gravel or glass to soften the hard edges of the container.

containers can help to establish a garden that fits in with its urban surroundings.

Strong materials, such as concrete, benefit from simple and bold plantings. Grasses have a particular affinity with concrete containers, particularly the blue-gray foliage of *Festuca glauca,* the powerful thrust of phormium, and I also love the silver of *Euphorbia myrsinites*. The silvery gray foliage of teucrium, with its sky blue flowers, will help to break up the hard line of a concrete container edge, as will the silvery feathered leaves of cineraria or a gold grass such as hakonechloa.

More recently, concrete containers have become

◀ A little imagination and these concrete circles are transformed. A couple of bands of copper wire around them give these containers an individual look. They also help to visually link the container with the flooring, which is made of rusting steel panels.

◀◀ A concrete courtyard with huge concrete containers gives the impression of permanence. This is a valuable, stable material for busy areas and when planting large specimen trees and hedges.

▶ A custom-made concrete pot decorated with purple and pink clouds is a special feature in the garden. The red-leafed phormium appears like a fountain of foliage.

METHOD

• This large concrete container is heavy, so make sure that there are two of you to carry it.

• Drill drainage holes in the base of the container with a masonry bit and place broken crockery in the bottom.

• Fill half of this deep container with pieces of polystyrene and infill with soil-based compost. Try to shake the soil down between the gaps in the polystyrene pieces.

• Plant the container at any time of year. Place the choisya and lamium so that they sit about ½ inch (1 cm) below the rim of the pot.

• Feed with seaweed fertilizer.

• Cut back lamium when it gets leggy. Trim the choisya once it has flowered to maintain the plant's compact bush shape. Eventually, the choisya may take over the whole pot.

shade-loving companions

This arrangement looks good in a modern setting and its fresh appearance helps to lift a shady area of the garden. I think the smooth surface of the concrete creates a good foil for the foilage, and the golden hue of the choisya leaves is exaggerated when set against this pale concrete surface. *Choisya ternata* 'Sundance,' a slow-growing compact evergreen shrub, occupies center stage. It produces attractive white flowers in early summer, and glossy golden foliage year-round. Take care, because very hot sun may scorch the foliage. The choisya is underplanted with *Lamium maculatum* 'Beacon Silver.'

PLANTING MATERIALS

Tall concrete container

Broken crockery

Broken polystyrene or similar lightweight filler

Soil-based compost

PLANTS

Choisya ternata 'Sundance'

Lamium maculatum 'Beacon Silver'

PLANT ALTERNATIVES

Choisya ternata 'Goldfinger'

Escallonia 'Gold Brian'

Jasminum 'Fiona Sunrise'

Vinca major

Vinca minor 'Variegata'

metal

The new generation of large planters is dominated by those made of metal, and new designs and finishes help the gardener to achieve contemporary effects and create lovely gardens where there is little natural soil.

The variety of metal containers available to the gardener has expanded dramatically in recent years. They used to be expensive and rare and the choice limited. However, the new designs are simple and understated, creating a range of planters that are helping to define the small, modern garden.

The boom in high-rise living and apartments with balconies and roof gardens seems to have fueled homeowner's interest in stylish metal containers. The value put on any private space means that people are more keen to use any outdoor space they have for eating and entertaining. Metal containers are one of the lightest planters available, so they are ideal for situations where load-bearing may be an issue.

I think fashionable home furnishing stores have also encouraged the use of metal fixtures and fittings for both inside and out, and metal containers match the current enthusiasm for a minimalist approach. Galvanized containers fit in well with the architectural detailing of many of the newer buildings that often use metal in their construction.

The natural sheen on metal containers helps to boost and reflect light, opening up these limited spaces. Reflected light on a balcony is subtle but important. Garden lighting has also created new opportunities, and the reflections off metal surfaces creates some interesting effects at night, adding a new dimension to the idea of a garden being an outdoor room.

▶ Modern floating stainless-steel containers filled with grasses, such as this lovely bronze *Carex comans*, look like lily pads. The reflections of the metal in the water make this material particularly appropriate in a modern setting.

▶▶ These huge containers are relatively light when empty and are easy to carry. Metal looks natural in a space that is surrounded by buildings and sky, or against the glass doors of a modern apartment.

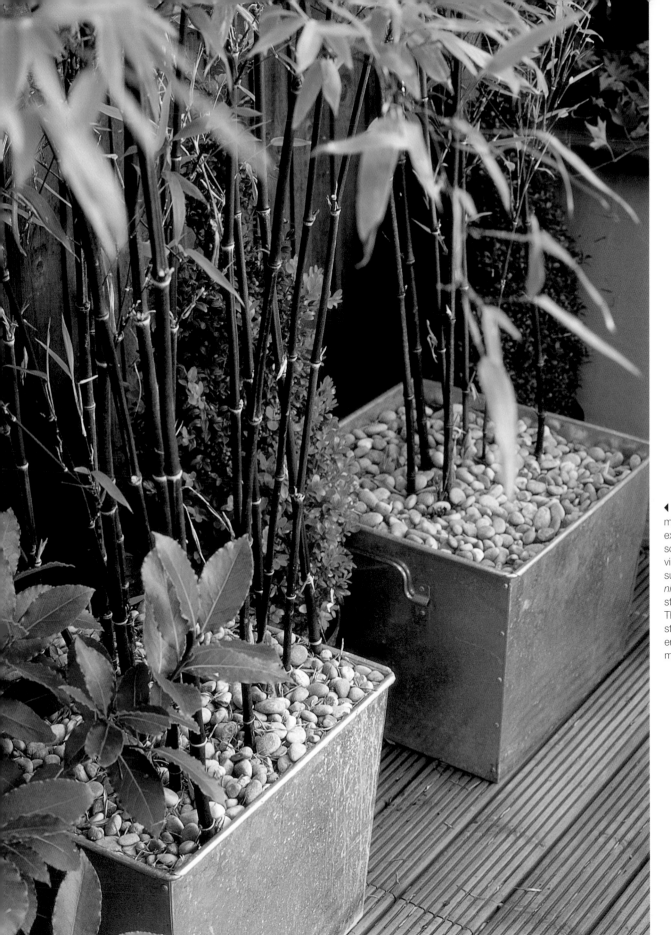

◀ Sleek galvanized metal boxes make excellent planters for some of the more vigorous bamboos, such as *Phyllostachys nigra,* the black-stemmed bamboo. The dark sheen of the stem looks stunning emerging from a pebble mulch and the metal.

Some metal planters mimic traditional pot shapes, but I think that these are less attractive than the simple squares, rectangles, and circles.

Different metal finishes are available, and the most common and appropriate for garden containers is galvanized metal, which offers protection against metal decay and rust and is both lightweight and strong. Darker burnished metal finishes are now available, and these give the container a slightly older, more antiqued appearance. Stainless steel is a heavier and more expensive alternative.

Large metal containers also provide one of the most cost-effective ways of introducing plenty of soil and plants into an area that has no soil without a major upheaval. Large-scale metal planters give the gardener wonderful planting opportunities—a metal rectangle 36 x 16 inches (90 x 40 cm) is ideal for growing such climbers as jasmine, solanum, and even wisteria in a large volume of soil.

As a base that offsets the plants, metal pots can look unique. Choosing a plant that complements the color of the metal is the key. Silvery foliage in galvanised metal can create a real focal point, while variegated thyme, pittosporum and myrtle leaves also look attractive grown in metal pots. White flowers appear clean and strong, and a shrub like *Cistus corbariensis* will mound to form a really substantial plant, with delicate white flowers and delightful aromatic foliage. Bamboos look thoroughly at home in metal, particularly the dark-stemmed *Phyllostachys nigra* when some of the bottom green leaves are stripped back to reveal the extraordinary lacquered black stems. Stick with the principle of bold and simple, but do not be afraid to experiment with new combinations. A large phormium looks stunning planted with some dark red nasturtiums, such as 'Empress of India' and the feathery silvers of santolina or some of the new lavenders. Olives are a natural partner for the galvanized containers as their

leaves have a metallic sheen. Matching the color tones of metal is challenging and fun—think of the metallic steel of an astelia, the silvery *Senecio* 'Sunshine.' I also love the yellow and green evergreen leaves of the grass *Carex* 'Evergold,' helichrysum, and the odd tight foliage of the whipcord hebe *(Hebe lycipodioides)*. But avoid using metal containers with plants in a wide range of colors—a reflective metal base planted with a kaleidoscope of colors looks too dazzling.

Modern metal containers can fit anywhere but look particularly good in gardens that have plenty of landscaped surfaces visible. The burnished planter often looks more appropriate in a natural setting, for instance an English-style cottage garden where there are more blurred edges—plants mingling with plants, informal shapes breaching the sky—where the darker finish feels far more at home than the shiny precision of galvanized metal. My own garden is a more eclectic mixture, and I

▲ A cluster of white agapanthus in an old metal tub is a magnificent display in the summer and helps to create interest in this small garden. One good-sized container filled with a single species often makes the most effective and dramatic planting.

have found galvanized containers a great addition to my landscape, fitting in perfectly well with terracotta, concrete, and stone pots.

Copper planters are beautiful when they age, developing a verdigris patina, but these are difficult to find and expensive. More traditional planters made of lead are wonderful but rarely available. If you are lucky enough to find one, they are worth cherishing, but remember they are phenomenally heavy. Here, the actual metal container should take the starring role while the planting is used solely to show off the container. Wirework containers that need a moss lining before they can be planted can still be bought, although more often than not from old gardening stores.

Double-skinned metal containers are available and these are useful in extreme weather conditions, because they provide some insulation against either heat or cold. However, I would suggest that in areas with really hot sun or freezing winters it is worth lining metal pots with polystyrene or bubble-wrap to insulate the soil and protect the roots. Any permanent planter would benefit from this insulation, particularly because unseasonal weather conditions are now more commonplace. Drainage, as always, is essential and most metal planters do not come with drainage holes, so drill out the base with a metal bit, and, if lining the container with bubble-wrap, make sure that there are holes in this plastic liner.

▶ A majestic, mature *Agave americana* complements the verdigris of a copper pot, creating a partnership that shows off both the planter and the plant to their best effect. Matching the textures and shades of color can create a display like a living sculpture.

▶▶ A small galvanized container planted with the autumn-flowering *Gentiana sino-ornata* makes a stunning display just as most of the garden is preparing to go to sleep for winter. A planting such as this is effective because of its simplicity.

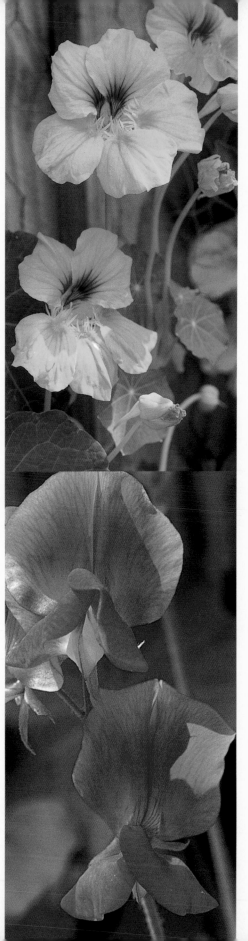

METHOD

• Ensure that there is good drainage and fill up the whole container with an equal mixture of peat-free, multipurpose and soil-based compost.

• Plant out in mid- to late spring in a sheltered position.

• Sweet peas are quite hungry plants and also dislike drying out. Keep well watered and feed regularly from midsummer (when they start producing an abundance of flowers) with a liquid seaweed feed.

• Plant the nasturtiums around the edge of the metal container. Deadhead the plants to encourage masses of flowers.

• Keep in a sunny position to produce the optimum number of flowers.

tower of flowers

I like the informality of this display, with masses of flowers and a lot of height and volume for a container-based planting. The proportions of this arrangement work well with the depth of the metal cylinder, balancing the height of the wigwam structure. Sweet peas (*Lathyrus odoratus*) are a delight in the garden and are among the most productive of flowering plants—the more flowers you pick the more flowers are produced. Nasturtium flowers (*Tropaeolum majus*) in clashing oranges and yellows spill out over the edge of the planter and flower with an intensity equal to the sweet peas. Black-eyed Susan *(Thunbergia alata)* would be a good alternative twining climber, with yellow flowers and dark centers, while *Tropaeolum* Alaska Series would make a striking substitute for *T. majus.*

PLANTING MATERIALS

Tall metal container

Broken crockery

Mix of soil-based compost and peat-free multipurpose compost

PLANTS

Lathyrus odoratus

Tropaeolum majus

PLANT ALTERNATIVES

Ipomoea coccinea

Thunbergia alata

Tropaeolum Alaska Series

A quirky container made out of a wide piece of bamboo, makes an interesting and surprising temporary display for a plant like golden everlasting (*Bracteantha bracteata*).

wood

One of the most traditional materials for containers, wood tends to be overlooked by the modern gardener as being too old-fashioned. However, natural or painted wood planters in simple shapes can hold their own in a contemporary setting.

The most traditional style of wooden containers are Versailles tubs, named after the palace of Versailles where in the seventeenth century they were used to grow exotics, which were brought into the greenhouse in winter for protection. I associate this style with formal traditional plantings of bay and box topiary, but these tubs can make surprisingly good planters in modern gardens. The main reason is that they are very adaptable, easy to stain or paint, and work well as an outer decorative pot for less attractive plastic containers.

Containers made of softwoods, such as pine, are inexpensive. However, softwood, unless it has been pressure treated to preserve it, is prone to rot, particularly in damper garden climates, so protect containers with a coat of wood preservative or paint. I often use wood stains and paints to help redecorate an area of my garden, particularly because my raised beds were constructed using wooden gravel boards. To create a harmonious effect throughout the garden, the same paint color can be used on a range of wooden containers. The grain of wood itself is an attribute, and many stains allow the grain to show through.

Another advantage of wooden containers is that they provide reasonably good insulation for roots in very cold climates. Wood is also worth considering if you want to make your own containers. Making large containers is easy, though once built, I treat them as immovable objects as soon as they have been filled with soil and planted. Ordinary preserved softwood is perfectly adequate, although using old, sun-bleached wood (similar to beach driftwood), with its silvered tones and splits can give real

▲ Versailles tubs are traditional formal planters ideal for such plants as these tightly clipped lavender. Staining wood, in this case gray-green, is one of the easiest ways to match the container to other garden features.

▶ A large wooden planter is big enough to house a specimen mature birch tree. Because of its weight, it is best to install the square planter in its permanent position when empty, rather than trying to move it when filled with soil and planted.

◀ A hardwood planter with beautiful grain makes a contemporary statement in this small courtyard garden. The compact pine works well, because it does not cover up the wood surface. The use of old railroad ties against the wall helps to link the planter with the rest of the garden design.

character to a space, particularly if it has a seaside theme. It can also add character to a contemporary space. Large, hollowed-out bamboo makes for a quirky, and surprisingly long-lasting, watertight container.

Beer barrels are now specially made for container planting and are useful in particularly busy areas where the container may need to be hard-wearing, for example, in driveways or at entrance and exit points to the house. They are also heavy and will hold steady in exposed or windy sites. When buying a wooden barrel check that the metal hoops are well fastened around the girth of the barrel, because when wood dries out it tends to contract. I have seen the hoops slip off and a barrel fall apart. Also make sure that there are adequately large drainage holes, at least 1 inch (2.5 cm) in diameter, and that the inside of the barrel is burned or treated with wood preservative to stop it rotting from the inside out.

To prevent beer barrels from looking out of scale when planting them, take time to carefully choose the plants. I prefer to use the large barrels, and plant them with something that can compete with their bulky proportions. Trees look good in barrels, partly because a strong trunk coming out of a wood base is like a horticultural sculpture. The beautiful *Prunus subhirtella* 'Autumnalis' has just the right balance to keep the display looking in proportion, or the beautiful bark of the paper bark maple, *Acer griseum*.

There are some sophisticated hardwood containers, such as dark iroko, that are beautiful, but they are expensive and difficult to find. Wooden sleeves to cover up plastic window boxes are also a good idea to improve the appearance of the house entrance. There are also forms of woodland split log containers, which are a good value but short-lived.

▼ With the increased use of wooden decking on terraces it seems natural to use wooden planters. These are like miniature raised beds planted full of herbs and are a simple and effective addition of the decked patio area.

METHOD

• Store the wooden barrel outside before use to keep the wood slightly damp which will prevent the display from drying out.

• Drill drainage holes at least 2 inches (5 cm) in diameter.

• Put in a layer of broken crockery and fill with soil-based compost.

• A mature tree sold in a container will almost certainly be root-bound. Remove the birch from its pot and pull apart the roots with your fingers to separate them out before planting the tree in the barrel. Water it well and mulch to suppress weeds and preserve moisture.

• In late winter or early spring, plant primulas and snowdrops at the base of the tree for extra interest.

• The snowdrops will re-appear each winter, and the clumps of primulas can be propagated by division in the fall and replanted if there is space in the barrel.

woodland coppice

I like the way the white bark of the birch matches the painted wooden barrel. Not only is this large tree firmly planted in soil-based compost, but visually anchored as well. This display highlights the value of growing a larger specimen in a container, helping to create instant height and vertical interest in an outdoor setting. The bark of the birch takes at least five years to show its beauty, so I think it's worth buying a mature tree for immediate impact. The snowdrops and primulas transform this container planting into a miniature woodland scene that can be recreated in even a small yard. Plant primulas and snowdrops in the fall to flower in the late winter and early spring.

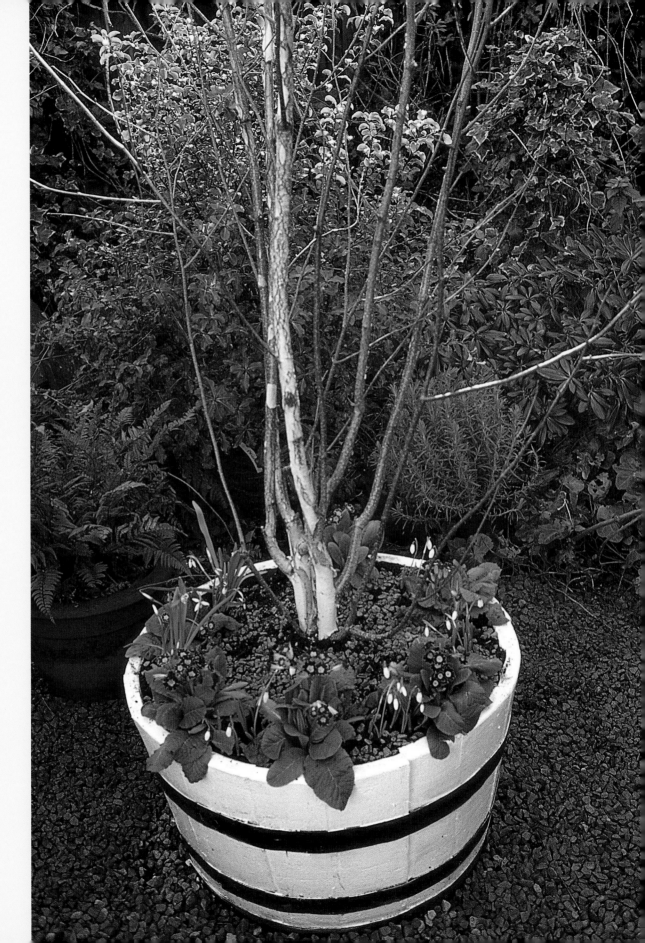

PLANTING MATERIALS

Large wooden barrel (unvarnished)

Exterior white paint for wood

Broken crockery

Soil-based compost

Gravel

PLANTS

Betula jacquemontii (Himalayan birch)

Galanthus nivalis (snowdrop)

Primula 'Gold lace'

PLANT ALTERNATIVES

Betula ermanii (white-barked birch)

Betula pendula 'Youngii' (small-growing weeping birch)

Primula vulgaris

Leucojum vernum

◀ I enjoy the simple pleasure of using recycled containers. Here, an old wine box makes a lovely home for growing shallots, sprinkled with some cockle shells. A box like this can last many seasons if painted with horticultural clear wood preservative.

▼ My garden until quite recently was a junk paradise, packed to the gills with reclaimed materials. The hunt for containers became addictive and though spectacular in season, it was hard in winter to keep it looking good.

recycled

Finding recycled containers is fun, rewarding, and good for the environment. A good recycled container can look marvelous in the garden and creates a really lovely display that adds an imaginative and unique edge to outdoor areas.

Part of the pleasure of container gardening is the hunt for attractive pots, but nothing measures up to the excitement of finding good recycled containers. With a little imagination, an old piece of junk can be transformed into a beautiful home for a plant, and you can feel satisfied that you have combined caring for the environment and your bank balance by creating your own unique display.

Many of the best recycled containers started out life as containers for either storing or transporting food and drink, such as the large attractive tins used to import marinated olives and olive oil and the wooden crates used to transport some of the more expensive wines. It is a good idea

to plant these recycled containers with something that reminds you of the origins of the product. Lavender works really well in old cans and wooden wine boxes, as do trailing geraniums, because both these plants are seen growing in most villages throughout the Mediterranean region.

In my opinion, the more delicious the product, the more attractive the container is to reuse in the garden. I like to use wine boxes printed with the words Chianti, Chateau, or Burgundy—all make delightful guests in the garden on a summer's evening, and what could be more appropriate than these containers for transporting foods being used to grow edible plants? In my own garden, an eggplant lives happily in a

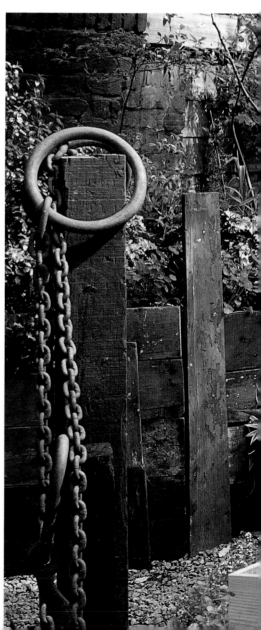

large olive container, while old tins of tomatoes are planted with miniature tomato plants. Because recycled containers introduce mood, texture, and color to the garden, planting them is fun and can be challenging. A really attractive rusty pot can be combined with rusty-colored foliage, such as *Heuchera* 'Chocolate Ruffles' or *H.* 'Plum Pudding.' These simple associations between a pot and plant also ensure that the display doesn't become confusing.

With most recycled containers, particularly wooden ones, it is worth remembering that their life is limited to a few years. Wood usually needs treating, and the application of a colorless preservative will help a wine box last longer in the garden. But the boxes were not built to hold the weight of wet soil or to be exposed to the elements for months on end. Also, metal naturally rusts, although oiling it with a natural oil can help to preserve its good

looks. Otherwise, lining metal containers with bubble-wrap *(see* Materials: Metal *page 68)* will prolong their life.

Illusion and fantasy can be explored to the limits when using recycled containers and by mixing in a few other quirky recycled ornaments. Toward the back of my garden, an old tea chest that I found in a dumpster makes a good home with ample room for a large evergreen shrub while a length of old chain, seashells, and seaside

▲ A real gem like this unusual pig feeder is worth showing off, not only for its beauty as a planter but because of its history. People like to guess its original use (they are always wrong), and planted with a mix of culinary herbs it is a beautiful and useful addition to the garden.

plants in old, weathered terracotta pots give my garden a maritime feel, although it is situated in the heart of north London. Reclaimed wooden planks and railroad ties extend into the area, and I have treated the wood with a blow torch to give it a scorched, sun-bleached appearance. I think this helps to fuse the seaside elements with the rest of the garden.

Used carefully, illusion can work well. I prefer to hint at feelings and not try to show them in full. Attempting a complete seaside scene in my small urban

paradise would be too improbable. I've seen upturned boats in an urban setting and they look out of place.

Unfortunately, collecting used containers can become an addictive habit. The more you look the more you find, and I have discovered at my cost that delicatessens and restaurants are always delighted to get rid of their used catering-sized containers! Although it's lovely having such an eclectic mixture of planters, take care not to overdo it or the garden will end up looking like a scrap yard. Also, in winter, when the plants have died back, the empty containers can appear a little forlorn, and there is no question that a poorly maintained garden with recycled containers looks more shabby than other garden styles.

Although found objects can fit in with most designs, the smaller the space and the more strictly themed that space is, the more care you need to take. An old object in a small garden can really stand out and become a focal point that can detract from the design as a whole. Make these containers more low-key and less prominent, and make sure that they merge well into the surrounding landscape.

unusual recycled containers

There are more sophisticated recycled containers, but often these can be expensive items to buy. Some are beautiful and can become an interesting feature, for example, an old metal washbasin or even a cattle trough will make a beautiful container. Plant these to highlight the container and do not obscure it by choosing to grow trailing plants. Chimney pots made of clay make a beautiful ornament in most styles of garden, whether formal or informal. I like the simple terra-cotta chimney pots that are free of ornamentation. These are challenging to plant because they are tall and narrow. My own favorites for these unusual containers are such plants as *Convolvulus cneorum* or *Thymus* 'Silver Queen,' which produce a shimmering silver effect. They grow best in a sunny site in well-drained soil.

preparing recycled containers

All recycled containers will need cleaning on the inside before use so that the soil does not become contaminated. Wearing gloves, scrub the insides with a mild disinfectant solution. When dry, drill several holes in the base so that the soil can drain freely and the roots do not become waterlogged. (*see* Care *page 132*).

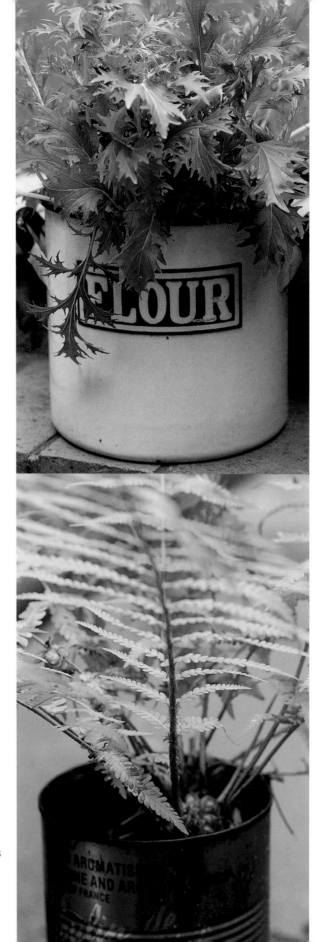

◀ Food containers, such as this enamel storage container, make great recycled planters, in this case for a planting of a mizuma salad. Food containers look far more at home in the garden than recycled containers that were used for manufactured goods.

▼ An olive can from the local delicatessen makes an attractive planter for a fern, bringing a bit of French culture into an urban garden. I like to highlight the beauty of the pot by matching up the metal grooves on the can with the patterns of the foliage.

METHOD

• Drill the container with a metal bit and make sure that you create at least six large holes, because yellow squashes are quite thirsty and greedy plants.

• Use an equal mix of soil-based compost and a little well-rotted manure, and add some well-rotted manure to the ground under the container.

• Plant the yellow squash in spring after the danger of frost has passed, in a sunny or semi-shady position, and mulch the surface to conserve moisture.

• Water well and feed once the plant is established. The yellow squash will not grow as big as one grown in a larger container or in the ground, but it will still fruit well.

• The container should help to protect the yellow squash plant from slug attack. Vigilance and petroleum jelly under the rim of the pot can also help.

pot-grown produce

This is a real eye-catching display that makes people smile, and it supplies some lovely fresh vegetables. This recipe shows the value of the flexibility of containers, using them in an existing bed to add another layer of interest. The colored mulch not only keeps moisture in but also looks great against the blue of the recycled metal bucket. In spring, plant the nasturtiums in the raised bed close to the metal pot. These are wonderfully hardy and will trail across the border, as well as mingle with the bright yellow squash flowers and fruit.

PLANTING MATERIALS

Recycled metal bucket

1 part soil-based compost to 1 part well-rotted manure

Mulch of dyed broken shells

PLANTS

Golden-skinned zucchini (Goldrush or Jemmer F1)

PLANT ALTERNATIVES

Chilli pepper

Strawberries

Sweet pepper

woven

Traditionally, woven wicker has been associated with rustic country-style gardens, but new designs and shapes have helped to update its image and make woven containers an attractive choice for the modern garden.

Hazel and willow branches woven into fence panels and flowerbed edgings make attractive borders for gardens, while containers made from these natural materials can introduce a relaxed feel to a city space. In my own garden I have some old woven containers under the stag's horn sumach tree *(Rhus typhina),* where I can go and escape from the telephone and fax machine and just listen to the birds singing.

Like woven fence panels and edgings, wicker containers are made from the flexible branches of willow or hazel, but they are usually woven into traditional basket shapes. However, the flexibility and strength of the raw material has encouraged people to experiment with imaginative designs that look more like modern sculpture than plant holders.

preparing woven containers

I like to use woven planters as a more attractive outer covering for arrangements planted in plastic pots. Like other wood containers, woven hazel or willow are prone to rot if they come into contact with damp soil or compost. To protect the weave, paint the inside of the basket with a clear wood preservative, then line the container with polyethylene sheeting, cut down to size and stapled to hold it in place. (Some now come ready fitted with a built-in plastic lining.) Pierce the plastic sheet a few times along the bottom to make sure that there is adequate drainage. During the winter months

or when they are not in use, try to keep woven containers dry by bringing them indoors or storing them in a garage. Keep the container off the ground so that it stays as damp-free as possible.

I enjoy the relaxing feeling of having a purely organic-looking container. It is the nearest thing to having nature create a pot for you. Like a bird's nest made of twigs and leaves, a woven container can look really wholesome. They are ideal for a little seasonal color, partly because they don't look like a permanent fixture. A collection of busy lizzies or cyclamen in the shade, a larger *Impatiens* New Guinea Group hybrid in a basket, or even a *Fuchsia* 'Thalia' dripping with orange flowers look completely at home in a woven container. I also like to use plants that combine with the strong horizontal lines of the weave, such as tall grasses, ferns and astilbe, which seem to celebrate life by exploding into the air.

Larger homemade woven containers can be created by securing together a small framework of softwood, onto which you can attach small panels of hazel or willow hurdles. This can act as a simple and attractive outer sleeve for plants already growing in plastic pots. It is still worth lining the inside of the woven planter with polyethylene to help prevent rotting, and a mulch of moss gives it a real country feel.

◀ This woven container has a rustic air, nestling between established plants and planted so that the shades of brown pansies match the painted wood.

▲ Hazel hurdles within a wooden frame bring nature to a corner of the garden. The hazel fencing panel behind shows the value of integrating the container with its surroundings.

METHOD

• Preserve the weave with a clear horticultural wood preservative (there are specific ones for garden use) and plant when the container is completely dry.

• Line the container with polyethylene sheeting to prevent the soil from coming into direct contact with the weave. Pierce the polyethylene and line it with vermiculite or gravel to ensure good drainage.

• Plant in a peat-free multipurpose compost, or if there is room, plunge the plants in their existing plastic pots into the container.

• Mulch the soil surface with chipped stones to prevent damp soil sticking to the container during watering.

• Do not overwater the plants, because all these species can survive happily in dry conditions.

• Cut off the old leaves from the phormium with scissors, and clip back the ajuga after it has flowered. If grown in its plastic pot, the ajuga will benefit from dividing in the fall of the second year.

modern
weave

This container with its sleek and modern shape, helps to break away from the usual stereotype of a woven container. The mixture of colored grasses and phormium create a lovely balanced display that would fit into most patio areas, and it will continue to look good year-round. Grasses are extremely versatile and easy to manage, and they grow well in the confines of a container. They provide the amateur or professional gardener with a wonderful choice of texture and color.

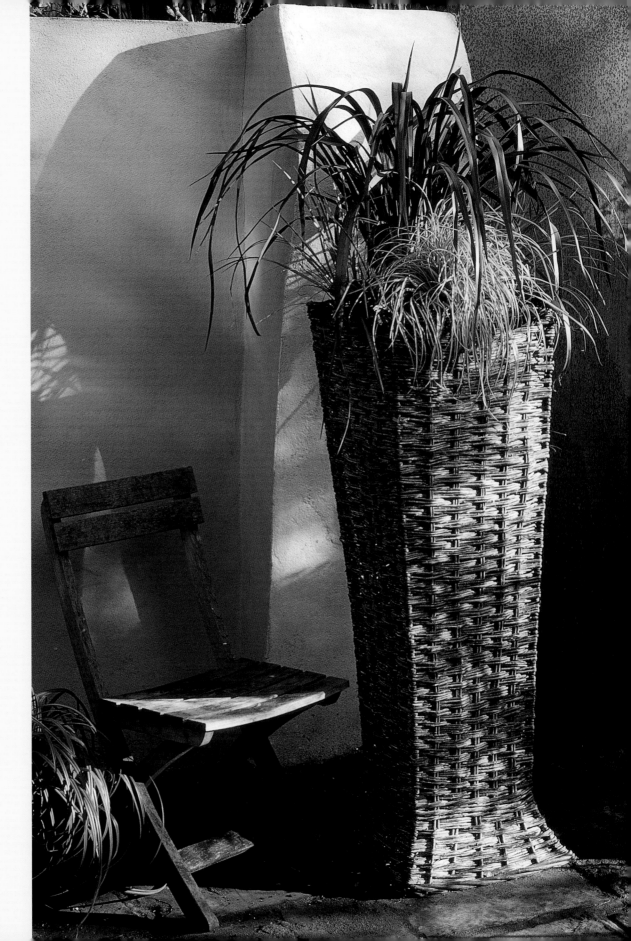

PLANTING MATERIALS

Woven container

Polyethylene sheeting

Peat-free multipurpose compost

PLANTS

Acorus gramineus 'Ogon'

Ajuga purpurea

Carex 'Evergold'

Phormium 'Bronze Baby'

PLANT ALTERNATIVES

Cordyline australis

Festuca glauca

Phormium tenax 'Maori Maiden'

synthetics

Unfortunately, some of the gaudy plastic and poorly designed fiberglass containers have given all synthetics a bad name. However, many are inexpensive and can make a modern contribution to the container garden.

◀ A group of fiberglass pots can create a fun atmosphere in the garden, and planted with easy colorful plants, such as chrysanthemum and kalanchoe, they are a child's favorite.

▶ A double sunflower (*Helianthus annuus* 'Teddy Bear') provides a cheeful splash of color and always makes me smile. In many ways sunflowers are ideal for a large plastic container that doesn't take itself too seriously.

Synthetic containers are those made of plastic or fiberglass. Plastic pots are incredibly light, can be inexpensive, and are easy to find. Although most people wouldn't be boasting about their new plastic pot, they certainly have a place in the garden.

My favorite are the industrial black pots used by most nurseries to grow plants. What you see is what you get and I like this utilitarian simplicity. They are not pretending to be faux terra cotta or any other material, they are just inexpensive, effective containers. My own garden is full of recently bought unplanted specimens, and the black plastic containers fit happily into the design. The larger plastic containers also have handles so they can be moved about easily. Sun, however, tends to degrade plastic, so these containers have a limited life of about five years. Colored plastic containers are more difficult to fit into a garden plan, but look cheerful when placed in a group in a courtyard or on a table top.

Imitation terra-cotta plastic pots are heavy duty and are a good alternative to the real thing, because they will not break or chip. Their light weight makes them suitable for roof gardens and balconies, but take care that they are secure in windy sites or when planting them with tall specimens. On the downside, plastic does not age beautifully like terra-cotta.

Fiberglass planters are a good investment, especially some of the imitation lead and metal ones that take a historical trough design and make it available at an

affordable price. I have been fooled into believing that imitation lead fiberglass planters are the real thing, although poorly made ones can look horrible. Large, custom-made containers can be commissioned from some boat builders who work with fiberglass, and they can be a stylish, if expensive, way of bringing extra plants into a garden where flower bed space is limited.

In a modern garden, these specially commissioned fiberglass containers have added to the choices available to the designer. Containers such as these have become a key element in the design—as important as the walls and the pavements—and are no longer treated only as an afterthought to be bought on impulse.

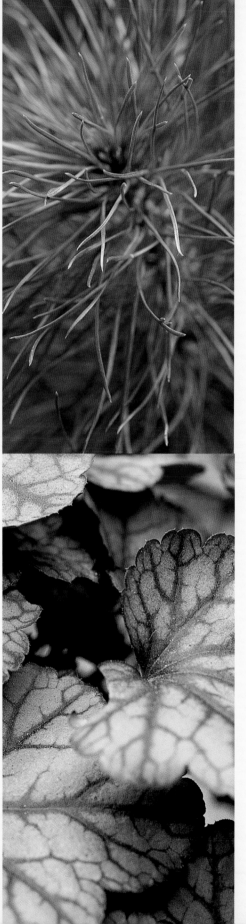

METHOD

• Drill a hole slowly in the fiberglass, taking care not to put too much pressure on the material. Use broken crockery to create adequate drainage and plant into a soil-based compost.

• Feed with general purpose fertilizer, although neither of these species need much pampering.

• In the fall, a couple of seasons later, take out the heuchera and divide the plants. Return only half the plants to the display with a little fresh compost.

• Top dress the pot with new compost mixed with a handful of bonemeal to feed the pine tree roots.

sculptural spikes

I think that pine trees make wonderful container plants and create an instantly modern feel. I particularly like this design set against a plain background. I deliberately chose a standard pine for this display. This species is *Pinus nigra,* which has relatively large needles and a relaxed shape. There are plenty of pines that would look just as good. Choose slow-growing, compact species that will not outgrow the pot too quickly. Pines are very adaptable and fit well in all types of difficult environments, such as windy, exposed sites. To create an attractive carpet of foliage at the base of the pine, I have used *Heuchera* 'Silver Scrolls.' This excellent plant has a fascinating veined leaf. The new range of heucheras is amazing—they are semi-evergreen and there are plenty of color variations to choose from.

PLANTING MATERIALS

Fiberglass container

Broken crockery

Soil-based compost

PLANTS

Standard *Pinus nigra*

Heuchera 'Silver Scrolls'

PLANT ALTERNATIVES

Laurus nobilis (bay) or *Olea europea* (olive)

Heuchera 'Plum Pudding' and 'Chocolate Ruffles' are darker-leafed forms or 'Amber Waves,' a gold form.

PLANTING MATERIALS

Imitation lead, fiberglass container

Gravel

Equal mix of soil-based compost and peat-free multipurpose compost

PLANTS

Buxus sempervirens (trained into a ball)

Curly-leafed parsley (*Petroselinum crispum*)

PLANT ALTERNATIVES

Ligustrum

Buxus sempervirens 'Suffruticosa'

METHOD

• Drill a hole slowly in the fiberglass, taking care not to put too much pressure on the material.

• Place a layer of gravel in the pot base and plant in an equal mixture of soil-based compost and peat-free multipurpose compost.

• The fall is a good time to buy a topiary boxwood ball. Try buying one from a nursery with the root ball wrapped in burlap instead of already planted in a pot, because they are less expensive.

• Remove the burlap and soak the root-ball for at least 10 minutes before planting.

• Plant curly-leafed parsley *(Petroselinum crispum)* in all four corners of the square planter. As an alternative, use slow-growing *Buxus sempervirens* 'Suffruticosa' in the corners instead of parsley.

fresh green square

This display shows the power and range of greens—the most restful of horticultural colors. Parsley is a wonderfully lush foliage plant and produces a sea of green from which the boxwood emerges. I bought the curly-leafed parsley in 2-quart (1.5-liter) pots and, when established in early summer, sank them into the four corners of the display. Keep the parsley well watered and fed with a foliar feed, and it will crop until the fall, and in winter during mild spells. Replace the plants when the parsley goes to seed the following year. Remove yellow leaves, and turn the display in the summer, because parsley likes a little shade. In the fall, top dress with compost and bonemeal.

site

sun

Planted containers can glow in the warmth of the sun, thriving in high temperatures and increased light levels. Choose sun-loving plants and a great pot, and you'll be rewarded by magnificent displays of flowers and foliage throughout the summer months.

South-facing walls, sunny borders, and bright blue skies are the perfect setting for many pot-grown plants, especially those that are native to the Mediterranean and Africa. Not only colors but fragrances become more intense in bright sunshine, and the garden feels more vital and alive.

Many of the finest sun-loving plants, including figs, vines, and olives, grow well when their roots are confined, making them ideal candidates for containers. In their natural locale, these plants can seem to grow out of pure rock. I have seen huge, ancient olives in giant containers and an antique vine with its stem gnarled and twisted growing happily in an old wine barrel. Figs undoubtedly fruit better when their roots are restricted, limiting leaf growth and encouraging bud formation.

Luckily, we are spoiled for choice when it comes to choosing container plants that like a sunny site. For large-scale plantings, choose such trees and shrubs as bay or eucalyptus or the magnificent

▶ Huge terra-cotta pots of *Convolvulus cneorum* flower magnificently when grown in a well-drained, gritty soil in full sun.

▶▶ An aeonium bakes in the heat of the day. These fleshy-leafed plants can withstand both high temperatures and drought.

◀ This agapanthus almost bursts out of its container and is one of the most rewarding of sun-loving plants. They seem to flower even more profusely when their roots are confined in a pot and they help to give this small garden a classical Italian feeling.

▲ Oleander is a plant that we're accustomed to seeing growing in the South of France. Planted in a container in a sheltered garden site, it can look wonderful and evocative. In cold areas, move the pot inside during winter.

▶ Nasturtiums are easy to grow and keep flowering well into autumn. These sunny orange and yellow flowers create a dazzling display that literally glows in the sun.

evergreen, *Magnolia grandiflora,* with its huge glossy leaves and heavily scented flowers. There are also surprises—the bamboo is a moisture-loving plant, but I have found that *Phyllostachys nigra* and *P. aurea* can grow huge in a large container in the sun. There are a number of different pines that are wonderful grown in pots and give off that fresh resinous aroma. When potting young plants that grow tall, make sure that the pot is large enough to hold the mature plant.

Many of the aromatic plants, often associated with the Mediterranean region, such as lavenders, thyme, cistus, sage, and phlomis, appear to produce more flowers, more intense aromas, and a better leaf color when grown in pots in sunny sites. These herbs thrive in the sun, and when their aromatic foliage is warmed, the fragrant oils in the leaves rise to the surface and increase their scent and flavor. In my own garden the bay tree that occupies the slightly shady position in fertile open ground is a huge, dark green giant with insipid-flavor leaves, while the one restricted to a pot produces far better leaves for cooking. Many other herbs like to bake in the sun, including tarragon, basil, and mint, and their leaves taste stronger as a result.

Most of the gray-leafed plants, such as lavender, *Convolvulus cneorum,* santolina, and artemisia, are adapted for growing in hot conditions. The range of lavenders available at nurseries provides the container gardener with an overwhelming choice of plants. Although the exquisite *Lavandula stoechas* types (French lavenders) are less hardy than *L. angustifolia,* I think they are worth growing. Use a free-draining compost and place in the hottest, most sheltered site in the garden. Their roots hate wet, poorly drained compost, particularly in winter, so add gravel and vermiculite to the compost mixture to improve the drainage.

Vegetables that originated in warmer climates, chili peppers, eggplants, and tomatoes positively glow when brought out into the sun, but during propagation

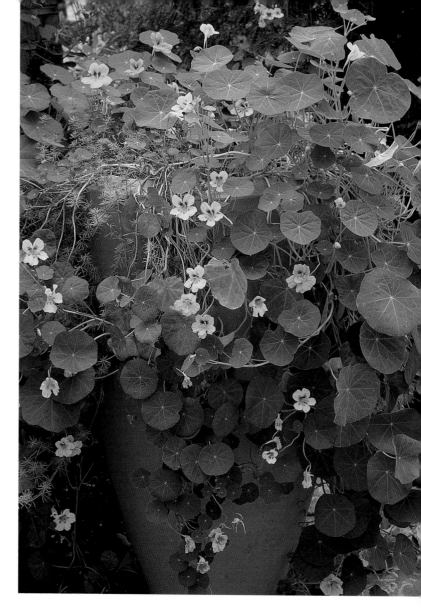

and cold spells, they must be kept indoors or in a greenhouse. Containers provide the gardener with the opportunity to maximize the amount of sun a plant absorbs, because the pot can follow the sun. My own south-facing terrace is cast in shadow by the middle of the summer, because of a large overhanging tree, so I often move my pot-grown vegetables into the sunniest place during the growing season so that they have a chance to ripen. My eggplants start in a protected corner site, and they always end up by late summer on the edge of the pond where the sun spends much of the day.

Many bedding and patio plants thrive in containers in the sun, producing a blaze of color. Every season there are new varieties available that promise even greater flower production. In the sun, verbenas, diascias, osteospermums, bidens, and argyranthemums flower to exhaustion. More traditional bedding plants, such as petunias, geraniums, and marigolds, also perform amazingly well, and their colors seem to positively vibrate in the sunshine.

In gardens where pots may have to go without water during a hot spell, choose plants that are drought-resistant. Select those with succulent leaves, such as sempervivums and sedums, or some of the rock garden plants. Palms with waxy foliage, trachycarpus, aeoniums, phormiums, cordylines, yuccas, and most of the ornamental grasses are the most drought tolerant. A mulch *(see* Care *page 134)* will reduce evaporation from the soil surface, and, if you are going away, consider installing an irrigation system.

Strangely, in dry, warm spells in winter plants in pots often suffer, because we assume that they have enough water and have stopped growing. Peat-based soils dry out quickly, and, when dry, are difficult to rehydrate. Water simply drains through the pot, so it needs to be soaked by standing the pot in water. Soil-based compost is better in that it dries out more slowly.

▶ *Festuca glauca,* phormium, stipa, and many other grasses enjoy being baked in the sun and are relatively drought-tolerant. I like to create a beach effect with some driftwood and stones mixed in with the containers and gravel.

▶▶ *Senecio cineraria* is one of my all time favorite sun lovers. It is incredibly easy to grow and very much associated with the seaside. Grow this silvery leafed shrub in a large container, so that it can grow into a mound.

▶▶▶ Here, purple sage is planted in an old French olive jar. I like the contrast between the warm ocher color of the pot with the soft purple tones of the sage leaves.

METHOD

• Drill drainage holes and line the inside of the metal container with bubble-wrap for insulation to prevent the plant roots from frying in hot sun.

• Pierce holes in the bubble-wrap along the base of the container and add a fine layer of gravel for drainage.

• To keep the soil free to drain (lavender roots hate sitting in water), add a scoop of horticultural grit to the soil-based potting compost.

• When planting lavender, gently tease the roots free of the main root ball to give them access to fresh soil.

• Water the container regularly throughout the spring and summer to prevent the plants from drying out. If you are going on vacation and watering is a problem, move the container to a shady site.

• Cut the lavender back hard after flowering, which will help stop the plants from becoming leggy and woody in subsequent years. Feed with flowering food in the growing season. Deadhead the violas, and trim back cineraria when necessary.

mediterranean metal

I like the silver-gray color and the soft texture of this display, which looks harmonious with the surface sheen of the galvanized metal planter. The center of the display is planted with *Lavandula stoechas,* which I like for its butterfly-winged flowers, aromatic foliage, and feathery look. Delicate violas provide color along the edge, and when seen through the silver foliage of the cineraria, bind the window-box display together with a colorful thread.

PLANTING
MATERIALS

Galvanized metal
window box

Bubble-wrap

Gravel

Horticultural grit

Soil-based compost

PLANTS

Cineraria maritima

Lavandula stoechas

Viola

PLANT ALTERNATIVES

Helichrysum petiolare

Lavandula angustifolia
'Hidcote' or 'Imperial Gem'

Lobelia

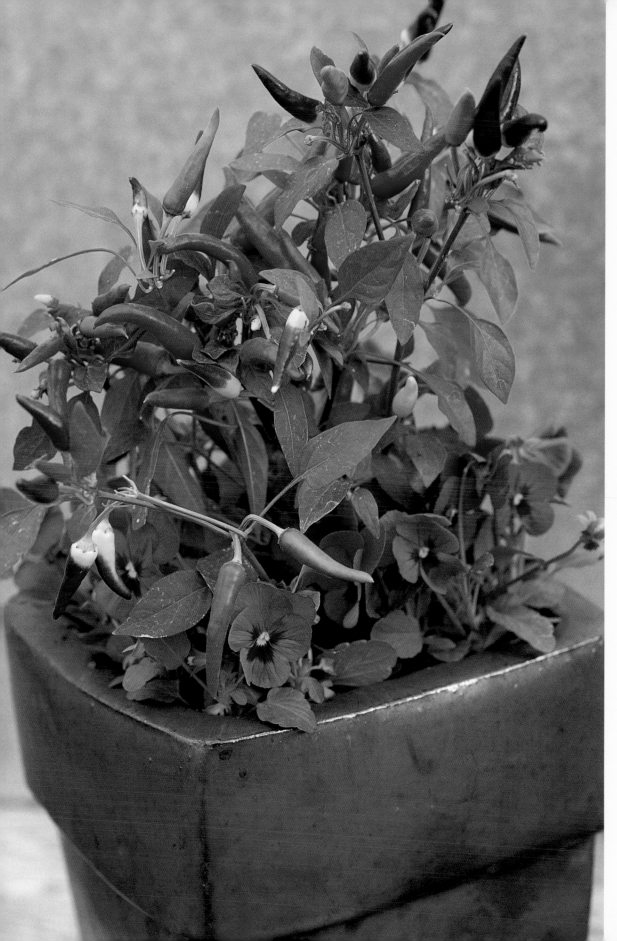

PLANTING MATERIALS

Glazed stoneware pot about 9 inches (22.5 cm) in diameter at the rim

Broken crockery

Peat-free multipurpose compost

PLANTS

Capsicum annuum Culinary cultivars bear hot-tasting, conical fruit 2 inches (5 cm) long.

Viola 'Panola'

PLANT ALTERNATIVES

Capsicum annuum 'Apache' (It performs well as compact bush and is a good fruiter.)

Any *Viola* species

METHOD

- Drill holes in the bottom of the stoneware container and add terra-cotta crockery to help the drainage.

- Buy the capsicum plants mid-season, when the weather has warmed up, because they are sensitive to frost.

- Plant this display in a peat-free, multipurpose compost and feed throughout the season. (Capsicum grow best in fertile, well-drained soil in full sun.)

- Put the container planting in as sunny a place as possible to encourage the green capsicum fruit to ripen, and water twice a day.

- Deadhead the viola flowers and pinch them off when they get straggly to encourage more flowers.

- Pick the red fruit of an edible capsicum when fully colored and use to add a hot spicy flavor to cooking.

sunshine spice

This display indulges the uninhibited pleasure of mixing plants that you would not normally associate with one another. Here, I have kept to basic color principles, making sure that the scarlet and purple tones of the ripening fruit, and soft gray hue of the container all work well together, with some powerful red highlights to spark it up. Somehow, I find a small display like this liberating. It enables you to get away from the more "usual" container-grown plants, and growing an edible capsicum in a pot, on a windowsill or patio, gives you a spicy culinary ingredient. Children also love this kind of bold and colorful arrangement.

A group of mature hostas in containers is one of the most glorious displays in the garden, challenging the myth that it is difficult to grow exciting plants in shade. Hostas grow well in pots which can also help protect them from slug and snail attack.

shade

There are plenty of plants that thrive in the shade, and planted containers provide some wonderful opportunities that can help to lift and brighten an area, creating lovely effects beneath tree branches, along the edge of high walls and in dark, forgotten corners.

Shade is often considered to be the poor relation of the sun and problematic for the gardener, but, in reality, there are many plants that thrive in shade and can be used effectively. In my opinion, there are few more beautiful sights than lush green hosta leaves brimming out from terracotta pots situated in the shade, or the glossy leaves and bright flowers of a camellia emerging from a dark recess.

Many of the best results in shade can be achieved by clever use of foliage plants. The great advantage of these mainly shade-loving species is that their period of interest is longer than many of the flowering plants. An evergreen, such as *Pieris japonica* 'Variegata,' is perfectly at home in a container and looks beautiful throughout the year. Some variegated and golden-leafed species prefer shade, because their foliage burns in the heat of the midday sun—the golden-leafed *Choisya ternata* 'Sundance' prefers shady sites for this reason. Also, many magnificent foliage plants, such as evergreen fatsias, are healthier when grown in diffuse light out of direct sun.

Not only foliage but flowering plants can excel in these shady conditions—the scented winter flowers of *Viburnum bodnantense* and *V. fragrans* do, while *V. tinus* 'Eve Price' has one of the longest flowering periods of all. One of my own favorites, *Hydrangea serrata* 'Preziosa,' can grow in the sun or shade and has beautiful pink lacecaps and red-tinged foliage.

It is often plants that thrive in woodland positions that do best in the shade. Ferns, one of our most familiar woodland natives, are an extraordinary group, ranging from the young emerging growth of *Matteuccia struthiopteris* (the shuttlecock fern) to the filigree foliage of soft shield fern, *Polystichum setiferum*.

The various different Japanese maples resemble a delicate lacework in the shade, and they have the perfect habit for a planter, staying relatively small while retaining a treelike shape. I made the mistake of putting a purple-leafed variety in too much sun, and the leaves became frazzled during a hot spell. Small trees, such as *Betula pendula* 'Youngii' can also help to brighten up a dark area.

Of the seasonal bedding plants, the best container growers for shade are begonias and busy lizzies. A group of impatiens can brighten up the darkest corner and flower the whole summer. *Convallaria*, the lily-of-the-valley, are beautiful plants for shade. Plant them out in open ground, then lift established clumps to make a display in a shallow planter.

There are degrees of shade. The dense shade cast by a sycamore or lime tree in full leaf is a problem at the peak of summer, because nothing enjoys growing under these trees, and, in these hostile conditions, I would recommend a tough shade lover, such as aucuba, ivy, holly, or *Prunus laurocerasus*. Most shade is, in fact, semi-shade, and often gets two to four hours of sun in the summer—ideal conditions for many plants. The area under deciduous trees often has plenty of sun from the late fall to the spring when the trees are bare, then the leaf canopy protects the area from the summer sun. These shady environments are ideal for pots full of spring-flowering plants, such as snowdrops, cyclamen, and primulas, ensuring cool roots in the summer.

In shade, flowers often last longer than in full sun, so take advantage of this. One of my container-grown agapanthus, which spends most of the year in the sunniest place, is moved into the shade when in open bud and lasts three or four weeks longer when in flower, because of the relative cool.

◀ A trio of ferns in recycled containers grow well under the dense canopy of a bamboo. Pots are useful in such small beds as this, where most plants cannot compete for nutrients with the bamboo.

▶ A shady woodland area in my garden is a lovely restful place that I really appreciate after a hard day. A hydrangea in the blue glazed pot flowers for weeks on end and impatiens are among the finest and most hard-working of shade-loving plants.

METHOD

• Place broken crockery in the pot base and fill with ericaceous compost—pieris prefers well-drained acid soil.

• Tease out the fibrous roots of the pieris to help separate out the solid root ball.

• Once planted, use a mulch of forest bark to cover the bare compost while the young plants are growing.

• Feed with sequestrine—a special food for ericaceous plants containing sequestered iron—once a season.

• Late spring frosts can damage the tender new growth of pieris. Protect the plants by covering them in horticultural fleece if a frost is forecast.

• After a couple of seasons, pot this display into a larger container. Remove some of the ivy, which tends to grow vigorously and take over the container.

shade-loving foliage

Shade is the perfect place for foliage arrangements, and this bright sparkling display can thrive in the gloomiest of sites. In my garden, I have placed this display close to an area where the ground is covered in ivy. It feels as though the display is in its natural home and has a permanent place, instead of just being a temporary visitor. It is often worth planting a container with something similar to what's already in the garden to help integrate it into the existing space.

PLANTING MATERIALS

Heavy duty terra-cotta pot

Broken crockery

Ericaceous compost

PLANTS

Hedera species
(Trailing ivy)

Pieris japonica
'Variegata'

PLANT ALTERNATIVES

Ajuga reptans 'Rainbow'

Euonymus fortunei
'Emerald Gaiety'

Pieris japonica 'Flaming
Silver'

PLANTING MATERIALS

Large glazed stoneware container

Broken crockery

Polystyrene filler

Equal mixture of soil-based compost and peat-free multi-purpose compost

PLANTS

Fuchsia molinae (also known as *F. magellanica* 'Alba')

Impatiens hybrids

PLANT ALTERNATIVES

Fuchsia magellanica

F. magellanica 'Gracilis'

Impatiens New Guinea hybrids

METHOD

• Drill drainage holes if not already present. Fill this tall container, halfway with broken pieces of polystyrene to keep it light before adding an equal mixture of soil-based compost and peat-free, multipurpose compost.

• Plant the fuchsia standard and impatiens around the base. To keep the standard shape, keep removing the side shoots with your fingers as they appear on the bare stem.

• Leave the fuchsia standard to grow in the container year-round and cut it back in spring to create a tight head of flowers. Replace the impatiens in winter with winter-flowering pansies or cyclamen. Feed with liquid tomato feed in summer, every few weeks.

cool green planter

This fuchsia is one of my favorite plants, and it has continued to thrive in my garden in a shady site. It is fully hardy and stays outside all winter. The peeling winter bark and bare stem have dramatic impact. From early summer through the fall, it produces delicate white flowers. Planting a fuchsia in a tall glazed stone container creates height for the graceful flowers to cascade down, so that you can see them at their best. This display also shows how containers can be used in conjunction with existing plants in the garden, and I particularly like making use of the powerful verticals in the garden, such as the trunk of the robinia tree to the left of the picture.

windy or exposed

Extremes of weather, particularly wind, can easily damage and dehydrate plants that are not naturally tolerant of these harsh conditions. But if you know which plants to choose and grow them in large pots that will not blow over, you can create a garden on even the windiest site.

There are plenty of plants that can tolerate gusting wind—just observe the bent-over figure of an old tree on a cliff edge. Plants can be tough, but it pays to know which varieties to choose for successful results.

Wind can damage plants in a number of different ways. First, there is the physical damage to buds, leaves, stems, branches, or trunks, and these can break off in severe weather. In cold weather, wind can reduce the air temperature and increase the chance of wind burn and cold damage. Warm, summer winds accelerate the rate that water is lost from plants and can cause the desiccation of leaves and young shoots.

Plants in containers are particularly vulnerable to physical damage, because of the instability of the pot, which can rock about in high winds. Also, because the roots are confined in containers, there is more

◀ A huge planter on a roof terrace provides ample room for wind-tolerant plants, with a few less hardy plants mixed in toward the middle of the display, so that they are protected. Here, grasses, bamboos, and phormiums help to shelter the tall stems of purple-flowering *Verbena bonariensis*.

▶ Agaves and cordylines with their strap-shaped leaves tend to be wind-resistant, but need good drainage to perform at their best, and they prefer a mild climate.

▼ Succulents, such as this sempervivum, in a tall container are very wind-tolerant, providing that they are planted in well-drained compost with plenty of gravel. The growing habit of these small, low-level plants protects them from strong winds.

◀ A mature purple phormium in a mild area makes a glorious pot-grown plant for an exposed roof terrace site. I like the way the grasses grown in the gravel around a pot of purple *Verbena bonariensis*.

▶ Phormiums and *Betula jacquemontii* are really tough customers and grow happily on an exposed canalside terrace. Birch trees create an excellent screen to increase privacy, and they grow well in large planters. However, these deciduous trees shed their leaves in winter but the white stems will still look attractive.

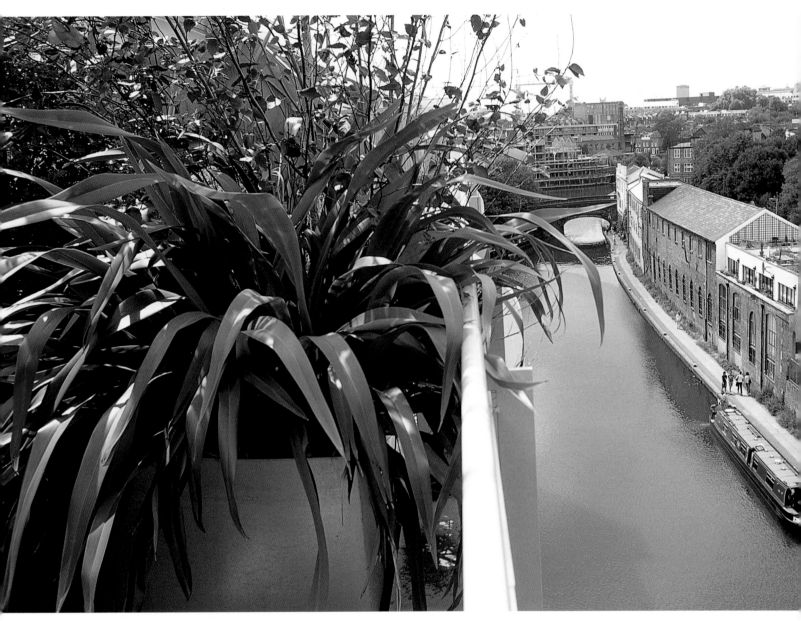

likelihood of the plant drying out, because of the limited reserves of water in the soil. In addition, plants in containers sit higher than those in beds, so are more exposed.

The most open position is a roof garden or terrace where there is little protection offered by surrounding buildings. Try planting phormiums, pyracanthas, escallonias, eucalyptus, and rhamnus—all

are tough evergreens that cope well with blustery conditions. In addition, bamboos, such as *Phyllostachys aurea* and *P. nigra*, are tough, although these can look scrappy in winter. In a large space use green phormiums to act as a filter and slow down the wind. I would also recommend some of the conifers, such as taxus, pines, and picea. These are naturally hardy, and their needlelike foliage is

wind-resistant. Many plants that grow near the sea are also excellent, including cordyline, trachycarpus, and tamarix.

Smaller plants are easier to find for an exposed site. Hebes are wind-tolerant, with the smaller-leafed ones being the hardiest, and olearias, spiraeas, yuccas, lavateras, and genistas, are all good in these conditions. Some ornamental grasses are also suitable.

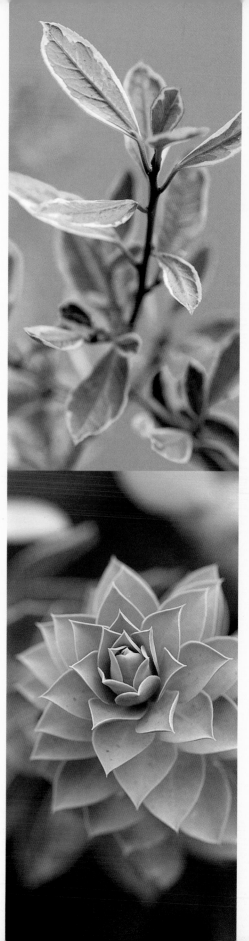

METHOD

• Cover the existing drainage hole with a layer of broken crockery and fill with soil-based compost mixed with a couple of scoops of horticultural grit to improve drainage and to help add weight to keep the pot stable.

• After flowering, cut back the euphorbia fronds. Feed sparingly with a balanced fertilizer.

• Do not allow the rhamnus to grow taller than 3 feet (1 m)—any more height and a strong wind might force the display over. Cut back the rhamnus in late spring to encourage bushy growth. Trim back long stems in the late fall at the end of the growing season.

wind-tolerant evergreens

This display provides an evergreen breath of fresh air, and the combination of plants, silvered terra-cotta, and shells remind me of being close to the sea. It shows how matching the pot with the plants is important—the silvering of the terra-cotta surface is perfectly matched by the gray and variegated tones of the foliage. *Rhamnus alaternus* 'Argenteovariegata' is a lovely variegated evergreen that is wind-tolerant. In cold areas, the plain green-leafed form (*Rhamnus alaternus*) is hardier than the variegated form, or use a species of pyracanthus. *Euphorbia myrsinites* has tough succulent leaves that curl up attractively at the edge of the pot. Other options to create similar color and texture to euphorbia include *Thymus* 'Silver Queen' and *Hebe pagei*.

PLANTING MATERIALS

Terra-cotta pot

Broken crockery

Horticultural grit

Soil-based compost

PLANTS

Euphorbia myrsinites

Rhamnus alaternus 'Argenteovariegata'

PLANT ALTERNATIVES

Hebe pagei

Pyracantha species

Thymus 'Silver Queen'

season

seasonal color

Bedding plants and flowering bulbs can be used in containers to create purely seasonal displays and provide a rich burst of instant flower color. They can also be mixed in with permanent plantings to help extend the display's season and then lifted out when past their best.

Managing to keep pot-grown displays looking attractive for most of the year is part of the challenge of being a container gardener. The smaller the space the more important it is to make every pot look its best at all times as every detail will be noticed. But, simply plugging a gap as and when it appears, or even constant deadheading and pot maintenance, is perhaps not the best solution.

Nowadays, the choice of seasonal color is vast, and many of these plants have been specially bred to grow well in containers. A display that has one main plant and space to add seasonal plant material can become a year-round performer. For example, a camellia shrub underplanted with polyanthus in early spring, impatiens in summer, and cyclamen in the fall and winter holds your interest throughout the year. Pansies have also revolutionized the choice of flower color available in winter. The color

▶ In early summer, a group of table-top containers filled with flowering bedding plants, such as *Bellis perennis* and campanula, can help to produce a dazzling display, which can be replaced later in the year for continuity of color.

▶▶ Petunias planted in a deep pot can produce substantial mounds of flowers—far more dramatic than if grown in shallower soil. Feed regularly with a flowering food to encourage budding.

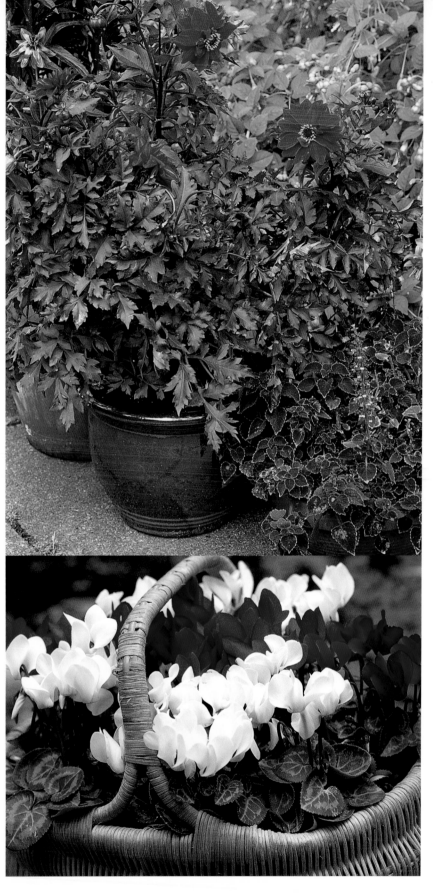

range is expanding all the time. My own personal favorites are the deep orange and copper-toned pansy flowers.

Containers planted with just one type of spring, summer, or fall bulb can also be a stunning way to add seasonal color. I am a traditionalist and like to grow plants in their proper season. Seeing geraniums on sale in full flower in early March feels fundamentally wrong, particularly when there are plenty of glorious spring bulbs to add color to your containers. A tub of spring tulips looks good not only for their flowers, but for the fresh green stalks, which build one's expectation for the coming season. A shallow dish of *jonquilla narcissi* look delicate crowded together, and summer lilies demand their own stage to perform at their beautiful best. If space is limited, plant seasonal bulbs in a plastic pot, and use the ornamental one as a "sleeve," so that the plants can be easily replaced once the flowering season is over. However, bear in mind that the space between the plastic and ornamental pot is "slug heaven," so separate the pots once in a while to pick off these hungry predators. Snowdrops fit into the winter bulb category, but will also multiply quite happily if left undisturbed in a container. Because their foliage is small and discreet, snowdrops do not have to be lifted once they have finished flowering but can continue growing among a permanent container planting.

For those gardeners who want low-maintenance container gardens, there are new varieties of geraniums that will drop their dead heads after they flower, although I happen to enjoy the simple repetition involved in this task. The range of fuchsias is huge, and some of the more subtle, elegant narrow flowers are exquisite for pot-grown displays. Petunias are often deliciously scented, and the trailing varieties, such as the double *Petunia Tumberlina* Priscilla can fill a whole tub like a colorful mop of hair. More recent introductions, such as *Angelonia* 'Angelface,' are summer-flowering, with fine blue or white petals. *Arctotis* (African daisy) make for a great display in themselves. I appreciate the combination of daisylike apricot flowers and silver-green foliage. New forms of nemesia are delightful, trailing slightly with bi-colored flowers. Try choosing varieties that are scented, such as *Nemesia* 'Karoo.' Bracteantha also have daisy flowerheads that continue flowering for six months, and, again are a wonderful feature in themselves. The trailing verbenas, and a variety such as 'Sissinghurst,' is superb, while the taller *Verbena bonariensis,* with its flat heads of purple flowers, is one of the finest of "interminglers" for a large planter, and it often comes through the winter unscathed. Other half-hardy plants, such as penstemons, make both fine container plants and are excellent in borders.

One of my favorite flowers—the sweet pea—can grow successfully in large containers, and they look wonderful climbing up a trellis or wigwam structure. Also, nasturtiums flower prolifically throughout summer and well into the fall.

Foliage plants, such as coleus, are welcomed to the range of seasonal color. Once common in the nineteenth century, they have recently been rediscovered. In a mixed display, I think their beauty is lost, so I prefer to use them on their own. A planter given the "coleus treatment" has impact and looks stunning. Plants with both foliage and flower effects, such as *geranium* 'Midnight Reiter,' which has intense purple foliage and lilac flowers, is worthwhile.

I have already written about using perennials as seasonal color, but I think it's worth reiterating that shrubs can be bought for container use when in flower, then transferred into the garden. I keep them in their plastic pot so that they can be lifted out again when required. Rhododendrons and azaleas can also be used in this way. They produce spectacular flowers for a short period, which look stunning when shown off in a glazed pot. I then lift out the plants from their container—with their plastic pot intact—and submerge them into the border until they are ready to flower again. They grow on to become lush evergreens while freeing up the pot so that it can exhibit another seasonal star.

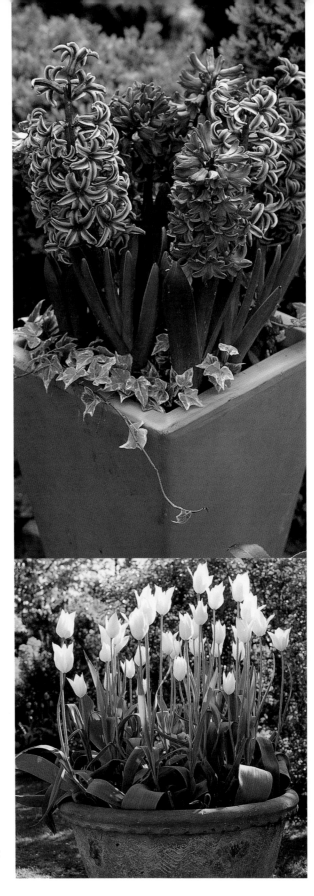

◀◀ I use the startling red of *Dahlia* 'Bishop of Llandaff' as seasonal late summer color to create a little fire and passion in the border. This display shows harmony with the red foliage of coleus and *Lobelia cardinalis*.

◀◀ Cyclamen can bring months of fall and winter cheer. The large-flowered forms are now bred to be more frost-resistant and less tender, with fine mottled leaves, and many have a sweet, subtle scent.

◀ I prefer to see hyacinths growing in containers rather than flowerbeds. Their upright habit seems to suit containers, and the pot height makes their delicious fragrance more accessible. Also, they can be lifted out once they have finished flowering.

◀ Tulips present an exquisite late spring show, not only because of their beautiful flowers but because they are a harbinger of summer. Protect tulip bulbs from hungry squirrels by placing a couple of spiky twigs just below the soil surface.

◀ An olive tree in the garden adds something magical, making it feel more special. Olive trees make fine evergreens that, in a protected courtyard site, can stay out all year. Placing container-grown trees in a border among established plants can add extra interest and height.

▶ *Nandina domestica* and *cryptomeria* are evergreens that give great displays for several months, unlike the fleeting leaf color of deciduous trees. These evergreen leaves turn a rust color in the late fall, and this stays all the way through the winter.

year-round color

If chosen with care, some container plants can continue to look fantastic year-round instead of being limited to one season. A framework of these displayed in pots can help to create permanent interest and will mean that you do not need to go to the expense and effort of changing the display.

In any garden I love to witness the different seasons and to enjoy the natural changes that they bring. In a large garden, the whole area doesn't have to look spectacular in every season but in a small space it is important to select plants that perform well throughout the year.

There are some plants that give shape and leaf cover through the year. For example, boxwood *(Buxus sempervirens)* will form an evergreen framework. One of the merits of boxwood is that it is easy to clip into shape. It can be sculpted into a ball or pyramid, or cut into a simple square. A piece of "living architecture" made out of boxwood helps to unite the house and landscaped surfaces within the garden, and it looks powerful whatever the season. Other evergreens that clip well are privet, holly, and yew, although it is worth experimenting with others.

There are plants that naturally grow into architectural or even sculptural shapes without the need for clipping. *Cupressus sempervirens* 'Stricta,' the Italian cypress, stands tall, presenting a dark outline against the sky. Conversely, the slightly amorphous mound of a *Genista lydia* will tumble out of a container, creating an attractive, informal shape, then will suddenly light up with bright yellow, pealike flowers in spring. The architectural silhouette of *Mahonia* 'Charity' is also striking and combines panicles of scented yellow flowers in winter with serrated evergreen leaves.

▶ *Pittosporum* 'Garnettii' is one of the finest of variegated evergreens – their leaves developing an attractive pink tinge in the cold of winter. At that time, I move this display closer to the house so that it is in full view. Being able to move containers around from one place to another means that you can alter the appearance of the garden throughout the year with the minimum of fuss.

▼ The cabbagelike leaves of *Bergenia cordifolia* create a ruffle of decorative leaves at the neck of this concrete container, while red cordyline leaves fan out like tail feathers. In winter, the bergenia leaves will also turn red, then the plant will flower in spring. The pansies are a winter addition to an otherwise year-round display.

Plenty of container-grown evergreens can look good year-round. One of my favorite, *Pittosporum* 'Tom Thumb,' is a dwarf form with dark purple foliage, and it looks at home in most styles of container. Sarcococca is an extremely hardy, shade-tolerant evergreen with tiny white-scented flowers in winter. Another worthy evergreen that has good year-round merits is *Choisya ternata*. The soft green foliage makes a good foil for other plants, it flowers once in spring, then often has a second flush in late summer. Added to that, the foliage releases a fragrant orangey aroma. The golden forms *Choisya ternata* 'Sundance' and 'Goldfinger' also grow particularly well in containers. *Arbutus unedo,* the strawberry tree, has good flowers, berries, and neat evergreen foliage. The smaller growing ceanothus are valuable, and 'Yankee Point' has the best habit for a container because it is grows to about 4 feet (1.2 m).

Bamboos and evergreen grasses are of interest because of their year-round color, and for their gentle, swaying movement. The lovely blue-gray leaves of *Helictotrichon sempervirens* are topped with masses of slender flowers that wave gracefully in the breeze. I also like the shaggy mane of *Carex* 'Evergold,' which always appears ebullient and cheerful.

Less obvious year-round interest can be provided by surprising plants. Part of my passion for agapanthus is that I like the look of the evergreen species in winter, which have floppy strap-shaped leaves, as well as the wonderful flowers and seedheads in summer and the fall. Purple sage can look sulky in winter, but sage leaves covered in frost is an attractive sight. *Hydrangea petiolaris* in a pot looks stark in winter, but has fascinating bark. *Rhododendron yakushimanum* has gorgeous pink buds and spectacular white flowers. I grow it for its dark olive-green foliage and its compact form that always looks good in a container. Olive trees themselves make wonderful pot-grown evergreens, provided the leaves are protected from severe frosts.

Tree and shrub bark can be a fascinating feature throughout the year—for example, the stunning bark of ericaceous *Stuartia sinensis*, as well as that of the many different birch trees and the maples. One of the best plants to combine fall color with another season's interest is the peeling bark maple, *Acer griseum*. Also, the polished peeling bark of *Prunus serrula* is worth considering, because the bark glows in winter, and this species will grow well in a large planter.

Fall colors are usually a more fleeting and less predictable attribute of a plant. In a windy site, I have watched maple leaves turning colorful one day, only to be shed from the tree the next day. The evergreens nandina and cryptomeria, however, will provide lovely fall effects that continue into winter. The fall is the season that also heralds the arrival of colorful berries. Pyracantha, skimmia, and cotoneasters are all useful evergreens with handsome berries.

Covering walls with evergreen or semi-evergreen climbers (keeping its leaves in mild winters or when sheltered by a wall) is often a useful way of greening up a hard surface. *Akebia quinata* is a fascinating evergreen with odd purple flowers, which appear in late winter and are delicately scented. The huge range of ivy is also well worth considering for their year-round coverage, leaf shape, and color. Trachelospermum is one of the finest of evergreen climbers, because of its glossy leaves and sweetly scented white flowers that continue throughout the summer. It seems to thrive when its roots are contained, which makes it well suited to containers. *Solanum jasminoides* is a semi-evergreen that needs a large container, because it grows so fast. It produces flowers that go on all through the summer and into the fall. I also recommend *Clematis cirrhosa* for its glossy, slightly serrated foliage and delicate, almost translucent primrose-yellow flowers in winter.

▼ *Trachelospermum jasminoides* must be one of the finest of evergreen climbers for a container. It has fragrant white flowers all summer, and dark, glossy foliage year-round, which makes a good screen. It is slow-growing, but you can buy mature plants for instant impact.

care

potting

The way that you prepare a container will make all the difference to how well the plants grow. Provide five-star treatment, which includes a clean container interior, good drainage, fresh compost, and healthy plants, and you will be rewarded.

When buying plants, look for bushy specimens that have not been forced to grow quickly in greenhouse conditions. Early season sweet basil that has been forced, for example, gets such a shock when it is put outside that it usually keels over and dies. You can recognize forced plants, because they always look slightly too glossy and often appear to be flowering earlier than they should.

With fast-growing species, I plant them directly into large containers (even though they look a bit lost for awhile) as re-potting large climbers and trees from a medium-size pot to a larger one is difficult to achieve without damaging the plant.

1 Plenty of gravel and broken crockery at the bottom of the pot help to ensure good drainage and prevent the plant roots from becoming waterlogged. With large containers, consider using broken-up pieces of polystyrene instead to reduce the weight of the planted container.

2 Carefully lower the plant into the pot, supporting it with two hands around the root ball instead of holding the stem. Fill in around the plant with compost until it sits about 1 inch (2.5 cm) below the rim of the pot. With a single specimen, take care to center and straighten it.

3 A mulch of gravel on the surface will help conserve moisture by limiting evaporation from the compost. It will also prevent weeds from growing. Ornamental mulches (see Mulching) can do the job just as well, although gravel gives a horticultural feeling.

Most container-grown plants prefer their roots to be quite restricted, so choose a container not much bigger than the plastic pot you have bought it in. Once you have selected your container, make sure that it has adequate drainage holes and put in a layer of broken crockery or gravel at the bottom. Choose a suitable soil mixture for the species, for example lime haters, such as camellias, require an ericaceous compost. Soil-based compost is heavier, holds nutrients better, and is more appropriate for permanent plantings, while multipurpose compost is lighter and good for seasonal displays. With most plants, I prefer to use an equal mixture of soil-based compost and peat-free, multipurpose compost and a scoop of horticultural grit to improve the drainage. With Mediterranean plants and others that appreciate well-drained soil, use more grit in the mixture. This will help protect the plants from water-logging and freezing in winter.

If the root ball of the plant is tight and compact when you lift it out of its pot before planting, tease out the roots slightly, so that they can start to spread out quickly and gain a foothold in the fresh soil. Plant so that the level of the soil is about 1 inch (2.5 cm) below the rim of the pot. Once in the container, water the plants well—then water them again. Freshly planted specimens need a drenching.

Plants that have been growing in a container for several years may need to be repotted to maintain their health and vigor, even if you have been top-dressing and feeding the plants. Choose a new container slightly larger than the existing one. Then lift the plants and brush some of the old soil out of the root ball. To anchor the plants, gently pour in the fresh compost around the sides, and press it down gently with your hand until the container is almost full to the rim. Move the pot to your intended location, then water well. Add more compost after watering, if necessary, and mulch the surface.

1 Use a power drill to make a series of evenly spaced holes in the base of a wooden window box. This will ensure adequate drainage for the plant roots. It is a common mistake to have too few holes, which can easily get blocked up even if a layer of gravel has been added.

2 Before filling with compost, place a generous layer of gravel in the bottom of the container, particularly if you are planting herbs, rock garden plants, or Mediterranean plants because they will grow best in well-drained soil.

mulching

Mulching is the icing on the cake, only easier. Nothing in the preparation of a container is so simple, quick, and rewarding. Mulches look good, they help the container to conserve moisture, suppress weed growth, and provide a slight barrier against slug and snail attack. I like to consider the other landscaped surfaces present in the garden before I choose a suitable mulching material for containers. In my garden there are seashells on one flower bed, gravel on the pavement, and a slate-covered raised bed. I use these same materials as mulch in planters to help integrate them with the garden. Mulches can also help to create a story or picture: seashells become part of a seaside theme; bark chippings a woodland, and shiny pieces of broken-up compact discs give a modern edge. However, take care—too many quirky mulches will distract from the containers and their plantings.

When mulching, always make sure that the compost is wet before applying the mulch, then the mulch will lock this moisture in. I remove the mulch every couple of years to top-dress the container *(see* Watering and Feeding, *page 137),* then either wash the mulch and put it back or use a new material. Changing the mulch can help to subtly change the appearance of your container without changing the plants. When a planting has matured in a container, (particularly a plant with a bushy habit) it fills the pot, and prevents weed growth and evaporation without the need for a mulch.

1 One of my favorite mulches is broken pieces of slate. This natural material is austere and works well in modern stone planters.

2 Seashells used as mulch help to create a seaside atmosphere.

3 Dyed broken shells are fun for individual displays, particularly if the color coordinates with the plants and planter. Many different shell colors are available.

4 Stones are a heavy-duty mulch. I delight in rearranging stones which shows how much pleasure can be found in very ordinary jobs when gardening!

5 Iron shavings are one of the more bizarre byproducts that are now used as mulch. In time, this metal loses its sheen which creates a rather lovely changing effect.

6 Dyed crushed safety glass from car windows make an excellent mulch with no sharp edges. The effect is contemporary and works with thin-stemmed plants, such as bamboo where a lot of the top surface of the container is on view.

7 Carefully chosen mulches can be worked in between plants with low-growing habits. Here, pink stones cover ground between succulents and create an interesting layer of pattern and texture.

watering and feeding

Watering is an essential routine required to care for plants grown in containers. You can forget to feed the plant for a season, and they may get a little starved but they won't die. You can skip pruning for a year or two and you may get a slightly oversized specimen, but forget to water the plants for a week in a dry, hot summer and you can suffer severe damage and, at worst, the plants can end up dead. Some plants are more tolerant of drought and can survive for far longer periods between watering. My own yuccas and agaves seem to thrive pretty well when watered only sporadically. But thirsty plants, such as pelargoniums, geraniums, and even lavenders, can quickly start to suffer from lack of water. But don't just assume that a plant with dried-out leaves is dead. One of my lavenders looked beyond saving, but after a thorough watering, it quickly recovered.

Watering containers is partly a matter of routine. During hot sunny spells check pots every day, and try to water the plants in the cool of the morning or evening to prevent the leaves from becoming scorched. Water thoroughly into the roots. Don't assume that just because the top soil looks damp that the pot is well watered.

During hot spells, I give my container-grown plants plenty of water, and I try not to always water the pot from the same side, even if access is difficult. When compost (particularly coir-based ones) get too dry, it can be difficult to rehydrate them. Containers that have dried out completely need a drenching, or, better still, sink them into a bucket of water and let them soak up the liquid.

When I go on vacation, I move containers into a sheltered, shady area, so that they are less susceptible to drying out. Setting up a simple irrigation system can save a lot of trouble, and there are inexpensive systems available at garden centers that can be programmed to drip or spray water into the container at regular intervals. Because I move my pots about often, I prefer to water by hand, but irrigation systems are useful when going away.

Overwatering can be just as much of a problem for plants as lack of water, especially during the winter when the plants are dormant. If the plant is not growing and water is not evaporating, a waterlogged soil can drown the roots, which deprives them of essential oxygen.

Feed foliage plants and leafy edibles with a fertilizer high in nitrogen, and feed flowering and fruiting plants with a tomato feed or one high in potassium to encourage as many flowers and fruit as possible. Trees and shrubs will flourish if given a top-dressing of bonemeal in the fall to strengthen the root system. In a well-established pot, I top-dress the soil with a layer of well-rotted manure every two years, or scrape off the top 1 inch (2.5 cm) of soil and add fresh compost to give the mature planting a boost.

◀ Basic watering aids, such as a plastic bottle cut in half act as a mini-reservoir for water, and help to ensure that the water penetrates down into the deeper root system of the plant.

▶ An irrigation system can be programmed to switch on and off at regular intervals, ensuring that watering takes place even when you are away. The water drip-feeders are staked into the soil and have to be lifted out and checked from time to time to make sure that they have not become blocked with limescale.

◀ Pick off the dead pansy flowerheads regularly to encourage new flowers. That way the energy that the plants would have put into seed production goes back into budding and flowering. Old flowerheads are also removed for aesthetic reasons, so that they don't spoil the beauty of the plant in full flower.

▶ Trimming box topiary by hand with garden shears is both a relaxing and rewarding task. When cutting large-leaved topiary plants, such as bay (*Laurus nobilis*), cut the stems instead of the leaves. Stand back from time to time to check the shape.

pruning

Trimming pot-grown plants once a year has advantages. It will keep the plants in proportion to the pot, keep the plants healthy, and increase flower and foliage production. Timing is important, because cutting back plants at the wrong time can remove the flowering wood and produce leafy growth instead. Plants that flower early in the season, such as flowring quince, flower on old wood and are best cut back after flowering. Late flowerers, such as caryopteris, flower on this season's growth and should be cut back early in the season. Mediterranean plants appreciate being trimmed back after flowering to stop them becoming too leggy. Cutting back also creates bushier specimens. A bushier plant in a container looks better and is more stable—wind catches tall, thin specimens.

Many of the evergreens simply need a light trim to tidy up their appearance, but if you are trying to create a topiary shape, they will need more attention. I find myself clipping my boxwood plants regularly, however, I find it relaxing to nip out new growth between my fingers. The slower-growing specimens, such as yew, may only need a trim twice a year—once in spring and once in the fall.

Dead-heading helps to keep plants looking their best. For example, geraniums look far better with their old flowerheads and stalks picked off. Dead-heading some plants, such as violas, helps to ensure that the energy of the plant goes into producing more flowers. It's also worth trimming back vigorous seasonal plants if they are taking over a display. Such plants as argyranthemum will soon recover and flower again and pelargoniums can produce a second flush of flowers if cut back once the first flush is over.

useful addresses

Al's Garden Center
1220 N Pacific Hwy, Woodburn, OR 97071-3616
Phone: 503-981-1245
Fax: 503-982-4608
www.als-gardencenter.com

Alden Lane Nursery
981 Alden Lane, Livermore, CA 94550-6307
Phone: 925-447-0280
Fax: 925-443-8512
www.aldenlane.com

Armstrong Garden Centers
(This is their corporate address; they are a chain.)
2200 E Alosta Ave, Suite 200, Glendora, CA 91740-4673
Phone: 626-914-1091
www.armstronggarden.com

Berns' Garden Center
825 Greentree Rd, Middletown, OH 45044-8919
Phone: 513-423-5306
Fax: 513-423-6733
www.bernsgardencenter.com

Bordine Nursery Ltd
1835 S Rochester Rd, Rochester Hills, MI 48307-3533
Phone: 248-651-9000
Fax: 248-651-9009
www.bordines.com

Calloways Nursery Inc
(This is their corporate address; they are a chain.)
4200 Airport Fwy, Suite 200,
Fort Worth, TX 76117-6200
Phone: 817-222-1122
Fax: 817-498-4504
www.calloways.com

Chalet Nursery & Garden Shop
3132 Lake Ave, Wilmette, IL 60091-1135
Phone: 847-256-0561
Fax: 847-256-4978
Chaletnursery.com

Country Market Nursery
51 Gettysburg Pike, Mechanicsburg, PA 17055-5602
Phone: 717-766-7993
Fax: 717-766-7999
www.countrymarketnursery.com

English Gardens Nursery
6370 Orchard Lake Rd,
West Bloomfield, MI 48322-2325
Phone: 248-855-9240
Fax: 248-855-0646
www.englishgardens.com

Hicks Nurseries Inc
100 Jericho Turnpike, Westbury, NY 11590-1063
Phone: 516-334-0066
Fax: 516-997-2532
www.hicksnurseries.com

Homestead Gardens Inc
743 W Central Ave, PO Box 189,
Davidsonville, MD 21035-1935
Phone: 410-798-5000
Fax: 410-956-2926
www.homestead-gardens.com

Homewood Nursery Inc
10809 Honeycutt Rd, Raleigh, NC 27614-9795
Phone: 919-847-0117
Fax: 919-847-3481
www.homewood.citysearch.com

Kathryn (Kathy) Pufahl
Beds & Borders, Inc
PO Box 616, Laurel, NY 11948-0616
Phone: 516-298-1836
Fax: 516-298-1834
www.bedsandborders.com

Martin Viette Nurseries
6050 Northern Blvd, PO Box 10
East Norwich, NY 11732
Phone: 516-922-5530
Fax: 516-922-3801
www.martinviettenurseries.com

McDonald Nurseries Inc
1139 W Pembroke Ave, Hampton, VA 23661-1119
Phone: 757-722-7463
Fax: 757-722-5274
www.mcdonaldgardencenter.com

Molbak's Inc
13625 NE 175th St, Woodinville, WA 98072-8558
Phone: 425-483-5000
Fax: 425-481-4970
www.molbaks.com

Natorp's Garden Center
5373 Merten Drive, Mason, OH 45040
Phone: 513-398-2550
Fax: 513-398-7072
www.natorp.com

New Garden Landscape & Nursery
5888 Old Oak Ridge Rd, Greensboro, NC 27410-9265
Phone: 336-665-0291
Fax: 336-665-9436
www.newgarden.com

Nicholson-Hardie
5600 W Lovers Lane, Dallas, TX 75209-4319
Phone: 214-352-1397
Fax: 214-357-7928
www.nicholson-hardie.com

Orchard Nursery & Florist
4010 Mt Diablo Blvd, Lafayette, CA 94549-3409
Phone: 925-284-4474
Fax: 925-284-7993
Email: orchardfirst@orchardnursery.com

Platt Hill Nursery Inc
222 W Lake St, Bloomingdale, IL 60108-1038
Phone: 630-529-9394
Fax: 630-529-3795
www.platthillnursery.com

Roger's Gardens
2301 San Joaquin Hills Rd,
Corona Del Mar, CA 92625-1195
Phone: 949-640-5800
Fax: 949-759-0619
www.rogersgardens.com

Swanson's Nursery
9701 15th Ave NW, Seattle, WA 98117-2315
Phone: 206-782-2543
Fax: 206-782-8942
www.swansonsnursery.com

Waterloo Gardens Inc
200 N Whitford Rd, Exton, PA 19341-2049
Phone: 610-363-0800 ext121
Fax: 267-200-0728
www.waterloogardens.com

Watson's Greenhouses
6211 Pioneer Way E, Puyallup, WA 98371-4954
Phone: 253-845-7359
Fax: 253-845-8921
www.watsongreenhouses.com

Minter Country Garden
10015 Young Rd N, Chilliwack,
B C V2P 4V4, CANADA
Phone: 604-792-3919
Fax: 604-792-8893

imported containers
Tuscan Imports Inc
www.tuscanimports.com

index

photographic credits

All photographs by Marianne Majerus but we would like to thank the following garden designers and locations for their help:

2-3 Mark Pedro de la Torre : 4-5 Inger Laan : 7 Joe Swift: 8 The Old Vicarage, East Ruston, Norfolk : 9 Old Vicarage Hill: 10 Mark Reeder : 11 Ruth Collier: 12-13 Michèle Osborne : 14 Gardens & Beyond: 15 Catharina Malmberg-Snodgrass:16 Bedfield Hall: 17 Joe Swift: 19 top Bruce Fursman: 20 Gardens & Beyond : 22 Mrs Ward : 23 Declan Buckley: 24 top left Terence Conran, RHS Chelsea 1999 : 24 top right David Viall: 25 Diana Yakeley: 26 John Watkins: 28 RHS Rosemoor: 29 Carole Vincent, Blue Circle Garden, RHS Chelsea 2001: 30 Schwebsange, Luxembourg: 31 Mark Pedro de la Torre: 35 Ruth Collier: 36-37 Mark Pedro de la Torre: 38-39 Coworth Garden Design: 40 RHS Wisley : 41 Declan Buckley: 42 Chris Marchant: 43 top David Viall: 43 bottom Pots & Pithoi: 46-47 David Viall: 48-49 Pots & Pithoi: 50 RHS Wisley: 52-53 Bourton House: 53 bottom 'Gardening Which', RHS Chelsea 2002 : 60 bottom right Michèle Osborne: 61 Carole Vincent, Blue Circle Garden, RHS Chelsea 2001: 64 inset Diana Yakeley: 64-65 The Flying Garden, design: Paul Cooper, RHS Chelsea 2000 : 66 Ward & Ben: 67 Nicole Albert with Gardens & Beyond: 68-69 Christopher Masson & Ian St John: 70 top and bottom Windy Hall: 71 Chelsea Flower Show, design: Stephen Woodhams: 72 Kim Whatmore: 73 top George Carter: 73 bottom Michael Clark and Simon Steele: 75 Joe Swift: 78 Adam Caplin: 78-79 Adam Caplin: 80 Stephanie Donaldson: 85 Simon Denman: 88 Ann-Marie Powell: 94-95 Paul Southern: 96 inset Stephen Anderton: 96-97 Christopher Masson: 98 right Stabredimus: 98 Adrian Gunning: 99 Lara Copley-Smith: 100-101 Ruth Collier: 106-107 Glen Chantry: 113 top Adam Caplin: 113 bottom Adam Caplin: 114 Declan Buckley: 115 right Michael Clark and Simon Steele: 115 left Joan Clifton (supplier: Avant Garden): 116 Gardens & Beyond: 117 Declan Buckley: 120-121 Bourton House, Glos: 125 bottom Malvern Terrace, London: 129 Gardens & Beyond: 130-131 Joe Swift: 134-135 Paul Southern: 134 centre right Anthony Collett 135 top 'Gardening Which', RHS Chelsea 2002: 144 Christopher Masson & Ian St John: endpapers The Chelsea Gardener

author's acknowledgments

I would like to thank Marianne Majerus for her inspirational photographs, Bella Pringle for her clarity, patience, and guidance and Maggie Town and Beverly Price for their wonderful design work.

Thanks to all at the Plant Room, Camden Garden Center, Clifton Nurseries and Highgate Garden Center, Priscilla Amos, Mervyn Reynolds and the team at Bypass Nurseries, Stuart Lowen at Ball Colegrave Ltd, Jim at Ball Seeds, Paula Pryke, Carolyn Hutchinson, Michael Clark, Lorna Harvey, and a special big thank you to Lynne and Martin at the Red Mud Hut.

Thanks to all the many people whose gardens were photographed.